S0-BEZ-983

Florida Firsts

The Famous, Infamous, and Quirky
of the Sunshine State

Beverly Bryant Huttinger

Camino Books, Inc.
Philadelphia

Copyright © 2002 by Beverly Bryant Huttinger

All Rights Reserved

No part of this book may be reproduced in any form or by any electronic or mechanical means, including information storage and retrieval systems, without permission in writing from the publisher, except by a reviewer who may quote brief passages in a review.

Manufactured in the United States of America

1 2 3 4 5   04 03 02

Library of Congress Cataloging-in-Publication Data

Huttinger, Beverly.
    Florida firsts : the famous, infamous, and quirky of the Sunshine State / Beverly Bryant Huttinger.
        p. cm.
Includes bibliographical references.
    ISBN 0-940159-60-0 (alk. paper)
  1. Florida—History—Miscellanea. I. Title.
    F311.6.H88 2001
    975.9—dc21   00-013077

Many of the designations used by manufacturers and sellers to distinguish their products are claimed as trademarks. Where those designations appear in this book, and Camino Books, Inc., was aware of a trademark claim, the designations have been printed in caps or initial caps.

Cover and interior design: Jerilyn Kauffman

This book is available at a special discount on bulk purchases for promotional, business, and educational use.

For information write:
Camino Books, Inc.
P.O. Box 59026
Philadelphia, PA 19102

www.caminobooks.com

To
Rhonda and Mike

CONTENTS

ACKNOWLEDGMENTS

The author thanks the following for their contributions to this book:

St. Augustine Historical Society
Janice Stillman
Mollie Cardamone, former mayor of Sarasota
Duchess Tomasello
Betty Skelton Frankman
Preston Levi—International Swimming Hall of Fame
Linda Barber Brown
Alice Syman
Debra Wynn—Tebeau-Field Research Library of the
    Florida Historical Society
Cypress Gardens
Jim Duquesnel—Florida Park Service
Julie Bryant—Brevard County Libraries
JoAnne Young—About.com
Jules' Undersea Lodge
Merrilyn Rathbun—Fort Lauderdale Historical Society
Jennifer Bush—Publix Super Markets, Inc.
Bill Green—Chalk's International Airlines
Naval Air Station Pensacola
John F. Kennedy Space Center
Ryder System, Inc.
Carol Hupping
Joan Morrison—Florida State Archives
Alan Bryant
Marineland of Florida

Florida was the first place in the nation to be home to European settlers and the first to be given a permanent name. Through the centuries it has been home to many historic firsts.

Many could not be included in this book. Although we know they existed, their origins are lost in antiquity. We know the first orange grove was planted somewhere near St. Augustine around 1570, and the first cattle ranch was probably nearby. The first horse in the New World came from Spain, and whether or not it came with Juan Ponce de León, as many believe, its descendants, along with descendants of Spanish cattle, roamed wild on Florida lands until after the Civil War. The first merchant, first physician, and first shoemaker in the United States undoubtedly plied their trades in Florida, but we have no way of knowing more than that.

But while Florida is the oldest state in history, it is the newest in development. For three centuries it remained largely a vast, uncharted wilderness. Heat, hurricanes, and deadly yellow fever epidemics all served to discourage newcomers.

It wasn't until the real estate boom of the 1920s that masses of people from other parts of the country began to look to Florida as a new Eden and started pouring into the state in record numbers, both as tourists and as permanent residents. The new influx was helped along by air conditioning, the invention of an Apalachicola physician. And when another physician, Dr. John Wall of Tampa, discovered the cause of yellow fever, it was the first step in eradicating an age-old menace.

You'll read about them here.

Today, Florida has the fourth-largest population of any state. It's still one of the nation's most popular vacation spots, and two of its firsts—a state park and a hotel—are actually underwater. But the state has come of age. As it enters a new millennium, its firsts include advancements in medicine, science, and technology.

These changes are all part of progress; still, we who have lived here a lifetime look on them with mixed feelings. In his book, *Al Burt's Florida,* Al

Burt says the state's early developers failed to realize that "natural Florida by itself was a powerful attraction and, if preserved, might be a better and more lasting investment than any fantasy ever invented." The old Florida, with its pristine, crystal waters, lush forests, and uncrowded highways, was indeed a high price to pay for luxury hotels, theme parks, and high-tech advancements.

But technology has an upside. We watch from our back yards as a space rocket streaks its way to another planet and are reminded it was our state that first sent man to the moon. And it will probably be from here that he will first be launched to Mars—and beyond.

We can't help being a little proud of that.

Old-World Firsts

EUROPEAN SETTLEMENT

The first settlement by Europeans in what is now the United States was made by Juan Ponce de León somewhere near Charlotte Harbor on Florida's west coast. The exact location is unknown, but the colony was begun 38 years before Don Tristan de Luna settled Pensacola in 1559 and 44 years before the founding of St. Augustine.

Juan Ponce de León, who had accompanied Christopher Columbus on his second voyage to the New World in 1493, established a colony in Puerto Rico and was named governor in 1509. After his famous discovery of Florida in 1513, he sailed around the peninsula and up the west coast, looking not for the Fountain of Youth, which historians believe to be a myth, but for gold and land to claim for Spain. Since Hernan Cortés had found rich treasures in Mexico, Ponce de León felt Florida surely held the same. He began making plans to explore the newly discovered land, which he thought was a large island. He would come back with an expedition, conquer the Indians, and return to his homeland with their treasures.

In 1514 he returned to Spain, determined to possess the new land he had found. Impressed by his discoveries, the Spanish crown gave him a grant to settle the Islands of Bimini and Florida and to establish a colony in Florida. He was delayed, however, by the death of his wife and the responsibility of raising their two young daughters. It was seven years before he was able to return to the New World.

On February 26, 1521, he set sail from Puerto Rico to establish a colony in Florida and explore its interior. He took two ships, 50 horses, livestock, and farm animals. More than 200 soldiers, priests, artisans, farmers, and monks came with him.

An Unwise Choice

Why Ponce de León chose the Charlotte Harbor area for his colony isn't known. From previous expeditions, he knew of its Calusa Indians, an unusually hostile tribe whose warriors averaged six feet in height; and visits to the territory by Spanish slavers had made them even more hostile during his absence. Soon after the new colonists went ashore and started to build houses and shelters, the Indians waged a huge attack, killing several Spaniards and wounding Ponce de León in the thigh. Terrified and frustrated, the entire expedition sailed to Cuba with its wounded leader, praying for his recovery. But his injury was too severe: in July 1521, Ponce de León died from an infection of the wound. His body was shipped to Puerto Rico and is now buried in the cathedral at San Juan.

With the loss of its leader and the constant threat of Indian attack, the Florida settlement collapsed, just six months after it had begun.

OTHER SETTLEMENTS

Like the one at Charlotte Harbor, the settlement at Pensacola was short-lived. When a hurricane wiped it out in 1561, the colony was abandoned and not reestablished as a city until 1696. So although both Charlotte Harbor and Pensacola predate St. Augustine, neither can claim its status as a permanent city.

CATHOLIC PARISH

The first Catholic parish in what is now the United States was formed on September 8, 1565, when Admiral Pedro Menéndez de Avilés landed his storm-battered ship at the newly named harbor of St. Augustine. Other ships of his fleet had landed there the night before, bringing some 1,500 Spaniards who had come to colonize the new settlement.

Father Francisco López, a Catholic priest, went forth to meet Menéndez, carrying a large wooden cross that he planted firmly in the sand. With banners spread and trumpets sounding, Menéndez, followed by those who had sailed on his ship, disembarked, marched to the cross, knelt, and kissed it. As Indians watched, the party of Spanish explorers then celebrated the first Catholic parish mass in the new land.

A Dedicatory Mass

The mass was a dedication for the new city, which was named for Saint Augustine because it was on his feast day, August 28, that Menéndez first

Pedro Menéndez de Avilés holds a banner (right) in celebration of the first Catholic mass in St. Augustine. This engraving was made from a painting commissioned in France in 1875.

ANOTHER CROSS

Today a 208-foot-high cross, visible from 23 miles out at sea, marks the Mission of Nombre de Dios at the site of Pedro Menéndez de Avilés's landing. It was erected in 1965, when St. Augustine celebrated its 400th anniversary.

DEBT TO THE CHURCH

Without the early records of the Catholic Church, we would know much less of Florida history than we do today. With 14 volumes of baptism, confirmation, marriage, and death records, they are the oldest manuscript church records in the United States. The originals are housed in the National Archives in Washington, D.C.

sighted Florida at Cape Canaveral. It also marked the beginning of the Parish of Saint Augustine, which has been active ever since. The landing site was christened Nombre de Dios—"name of God"—and retains that name today. On the site, the Spaniards built the first Christian mission for the North American Indians and from there carried Christianity into the interior, to as far north as Virginia and as far west as Texas. Some 26,000 Indians were converted to Catholicism, which became the dominant religion in Florida and remained so for 200 years.

PERMANENT CITY

By 1565, two small settlements by the Spanish and one by the French had come and gone in Florida. In St. Augustine, however, Spanish settlers had

A quiet St. Augustine street looks much as it did in the 16th century. *Courtesy of the Florida State Archives*

built a fort, a hospital, a church, and over 100 houses and shops. By the time English pilgrims landed at Plymouth Rock in 1620, St. Augustine had already been home to two generations of Floridians. It is the nation's first permanent city.

Along with the rest of Florida, St. Augustine was a possession of Spain. With the exception of a 21-year period around the time of the American Revolution when Florida belonged to England, it remained under Spanish rule for $2\frac{1}{2}$ centuries.

The city's past can be seen today in its narrow streets, historic buildings, and majestic, old homes with overhanging balconies. A walk through the downtown district gives visitors a feeling of being transported through different eras. Facing the first public town square in the United States, built by the Spanish in 1598, are mammoth hotels from the 19th century, erected when the town was a winter resort for wealthy northerners.

Fight for the "Jewel"

St. Augustine has been called "the jewel in Florida's crown." Through a long history of hardships and setbacks, it has often had to struggle to survive. Over the centuries, several nations fought to possess it. In 1586, the town was attacked and burned by English corsair Sir Francis Drake. In 1668, it was plundered by the pirate Captain John Davis, who killed 60 residents. When the English established 13 colonies to the north in the 1600s, St. Augustine's citizens were forced to build an enormous fort, Castillo de San Marcos, to ward off their attacks.

In 1821, Spain ceded Florida to the United States. In a colorful military ceremony on July 10 of that year, American troops took possession of the territory. But St. Augustine's woes were far from over. That year, many newcomers died in a yellow fever epidemic, and Indian uprisings, which led to the Seminole War of 1836, brought a halt to economic development. St. Augustine, which had been the capital of East Florida after the British divided Florida into two parts (Pensacola served as the capital of West Florida), lost this status when the new town of Tallahassee became the site of Florida's territorial government in 1824.

Statehood

By 1845, when Florida became a state, St. Augustine's citizens had begun to rebuild, and the town was starting to rebound and prosper. But prosperity came to a halt when the Civil War broke out in 1861. Union troops occupied the coastal city for nearly the entire war. Once the war ended in 1865, Florida began to attract speculators, land developers, and a trickle of visitors seeking respite from harsh northern winters. Since Florida was still largely a vast, unexplored region and only the northern part of the state was accessible by any kind of land transportation, St. Augustine was the logical choice to become its first winter resort. When Henry Flagler, a partner of John D. Rockefeller's in Standard Oil, took his ailing wife there in 1885, he could see the town's potential. With his vast fortune, he extended his railroad south from Jacksonville and built two lavish hotels, a two-story railroad depot, a hospital, a city hall, and several churches.

What with all the changes made by all the different groups and nationalities that have inhabited it, St. Augustine exhibits a unique character. Today it has a population of 12,000, with residential growth mainly in the outlying areas. The historic district still looks much as it did centuries ago.

☀ To Visit: St. Augustine

St. Augustine is 35 miles south of Jacksonville on U.S. Route 1. It can be reached by taking Interstate 95 to Exit 95. For information about tours of the city or visits to its many historic attractions, call 1-800-OLD CITY.

FAMILY

While Americans often consider their "first family" to be the one that lives in the White House, looking farther south might be more realistic. The Solana family of Florida has the distinction of being the first documented family in the United States.

Today, the St. Augustine telephone book lists about 35 Solanas or Solanos. (No one knows why some chose the variant spelling.) In a state known for transience, where two out of three residents were born someplace else, the Solanas have remained for more than 400 years. Several thousand direct descendants of Vincente and Maria Solana live in Florida today, many in or near St. Augustine, where Vincente and Maria took their vows in 1594. Theirs was the first documented marriage of European immigrants to the New World.

Not much is known of that first couple, except that they came from the valley of Solana, in the kingdom of Navarre, in Spain. But through the centuries, their descendants have figured prominently in the settling and development of Florida. Early family members served as scribe and notary

Mateo Simeon Solana was the grandson of Manuel Lorenzo Solana, the only family member who stayed in St. Augustine during the British period. This photograph was taken around 1910. *Courtesy of Linda Barber Brown*

to the governor, as deputy governor of Apalachee, as admiral and commander of a Spanish fleet, as a corporal, a sergeant major, a mapmaker, and a priest. They hunted, fished, raised cattle, and grew citrus. They raised their families and found their livelihoods in the Florida wilderness.

Exodus to Cuba

When Florida came under British rule in 1763, most of the Spaniards left for Cuba, which Spain had regained from England in return for Florida. A few, including just one member of the Solana family, stayed behind to gather horses and cattle and settle the affairs of the departing Spanish. Manuel Lorenzo Solana, a mounted dragoon, was 23 years old and an eighth-generation descendant of Vincente and Maria.

Descendants of Vincente and Maria Solana, who wed in 1594, pose at their family reunion near St. Augustine. *Courtesy of Linda Barber Brown*

Although his mother and four siblings left for Havana, Manuel stayed in St. Augustine to face an uncertain future under British rule. He became a prosperous and influential citizen, and his name is recorded in many documents of the time. The Spanish census of 1787 lists him as an owner of 76 horses. He also owned slaves, cattle, riverfront property, and several homes. One of them, Casa de Solana, was built in 1763 and still stands at 21 Aviles Street in St. Augustine, where it serves as a bed and breakfast. By the time of his death in 1821, Manuel had seen three flags raised over Florida—Spanish, British, and American.

A Direct Line

Manuel married twice and had 12 children. Several died in childhood, possibly because of a smallpox epidemic. However, others lived to produce many more offspring. Most of today's St. Augustine Solanas are descended from Manuel, and it is through him that they can claim an unbroken

The Solana family coat of arms. *Courtesy of Linda Barber Brown*

ARMAS DE SOLANA

line in Florida from Vincente and Maria Solana. Others are descended from family members who returned to Florida when it again came under Spanish rule in 1784.

Today, many descendants of Vincente and Maria Solana own farms and cattle ranches, just as their forebears did. They have been soldiers, merchants, landowners, and clergymen. Some, including a NASA space scientist, are involved in professions unknown in their ancestors' day. Each year in April they hold a reunion near St. Augustine.

By 1668, the people of St. Augustine had already built nine wooden forts to defend their city, the primary port in the trade route to Europe and the Gulf Stream. That year, following a vicious pirate attack, Queen Regent Mariana of Spain announced that a more durable fort would be built to defend the city and its port. In 1672, construction began on Castillo de San Marcos, the nation's first masonry fortress.

The walls were to be made of a local stone called *coquina*, which means "little shells" (the stone is made up of the bonded shells of dead shellfish). The coquina was quarried from nearby Anastasia Island and ferried across the bay to the construction site. In an area now used for the Castillo's parking lot, stonemasons from Havana, Cuba, made blocks from the tiny shells. Mortar was produced from sand, fresh water, and lime, a fine white powder made from oyster shells. The fort was finished in 1695 and boasted walls that were 9 to 19 feet thick.

Castillo de San Marcos protected the Florida coast for two centuries. *Courtesy of the Florida State Archives*

It soon became evident that the coquina walls had a decided advantage: they were impenetrable by the enemy's artillery. When the British bombarded the fort in 1702 and 1704, the huge walls simply absorbed the cannonballs, which remain embedded in them today.

A Violent History

Assaults began while the fort was still under construction and continued for almost a century. Many flags have flown over Castillo de San Marcos in its long history, including those of Spain, Great Britain, and the United States. When the British occupied the fortress, they Anglicized the name to Fort St. Marks. When Florida was returned to the Spanish, they restored the original name. In 1825, under United States ownership, it became Fort Marion. The fort became a national monument in 1924 and regained its original name in 1942. But changes in ownership came about only through military agreement or political treaty. The fort has never been taken by force.

While marauding invaders failed to destroy Castillo de San Marcos, 300 years of heat, humidity, hurricanes, and salt water have threatened to do just that. A massive, $3 million renovation began in the fall of 2000.

 To Visit: Castillo de San Marcos

Castillo de San Marcos is on Highway A1A at the north end of the Old City area in downtown St. Augustine, just north of the Bridge of Lions.

Castillo de San Marcos
1 South Castillo Drive
St. Augustine, FL 32084
904-829-6506
Hours: Monday-Friday, 8:45 A.M.-4:45 P.M.; Saturday-Sunday, 8:45 A.M.-6 P.M. (5:45 P.M. Labor Day to Memorial Day)
Closed Christmas.
Admission charged.

MEDIEVAL CASTLE

Castillo de San Marcos, complete with moat and drawbridge, is the only medieval castle in North America.

HOSPITAL

The first hospital in the United States, Nuestra Señora de la Soledad—Our Lady of Solitude—was built in St. Augustine in 1598. With only six beds, it was little more than a lean-to against a church wall. Nonetheless, when a fever swept the town, the small hospital helped save many lives, not only of Spanish settlers, but of Indians and slaves as well.

The next year, the building was appropriated to house some Franciscan friars whose monastery had burned. Governor Gonzalo Méndez de Canco, seeing the need for another hospital, built one at his own expense in a different location. The site proved unsatisfactory, so when the friars moved out six years later, the patients were moved back to the original hospital, which had been enlarged. Nuestra Señora de la Soledad remained a hospital for 150 years.

When Spaniards returned to Florida in the late 1700s after 21 years of rule by Great Britain, they found that the hospital had been gutted by the departing British. According to the royal engineer, Mariano de la Rocque, it was reduced to a "useless pile of masonry."

INTEGRATED PUBLIC SCHOOL

Long before anyone heard of civil rights, Florida had a public school where whites and blacks were educated together peaceably.

In 1778, the Spanish government transferred Father Thomas Hasset from Philadelphia, where he was in charge of the city's Catholic schools, to St. Augustine. Father Hasset would serve as the parish priest and would be responsible for organizing and directing schools in his jurisdiction. When the Spaniards returned to Florida from Cuba in 1783, the Spanish crown appointed Manuel de Zespédes governor of Florida and instructed him to provide education throughout the province.

In 1786, the Spanish king's dream of a free public school in the New World became a reality. It was organized and run by Father Hasset and became known as Father Hasset's School. By this time, St. Augustine had become something of a melting pot. British rule had just ended, and Spaniards who had lived in Cuba for 21 years were returning to the city. Italians, Greeks, and Minorcans were now living there, as were blacks who had fled the American colonies to escape slavery.

A Free School

The school was free, and children of all backgrounds were eligible to attend. However, since it was customary for upper-class boys to be taught at home by private tutors, the pupils actually came from the lower and middle classes. And there were no female students; the king was not in favor of education for girls, at least not in a coeducational setting.

Francisco Troconis, chaplain of the Royal Hospital, was appointed the first schoolmaster. He clearly was not happy with the job or with his salary of eight pesos (about eight dollars) a month. He longed to return to his native city of Havana, Cuba, where he hoped to obtain an appointment in the cathedral. After four months, he was pleading with the governor to find a successor. A year and a half later, after advancing the argument that he had young nieces in Havana who needed his protection, Troconis was granted a two-month leave of absence to return to Cuba.

When Troconis didn't return after the two months, Father Hasset set out to find a new schoolmaster. At the salary he was authorized to pay, it

LOCATION

Father Hasset's School was located on St. George Street at the south corner of Bridge Street in St. Augustine, on property now owned by the Trinity Episcopal Church.

proved to be a daunting task. Fifty pages of correspondence about Hasset's attempts to solve the problem are on file in the Library of Congress. Records show that he eventually did find a successor to Troconis, but apparently the new schoolmaster didn't work out either. It is unknown whether Troconis ever returned to St. Augustine or how long the school survived.

WAR

In addition to founding the city of St. Augustine, Pedro Menéndez de Avilés was assigned a second task by Spain's King Philip II. He was told to "drive out any corsairs or settlers of other nations if they should be found in Florida." This led to the first war waged in what is now the United States.

A colony of French Huguenots, who had fled persecution in France for embracing the Lutheran religion, was encamped in Fort Caroline at St. John's Bluff, near present-day Jacksonville. Menéndez deemed it his duty to drive out the heretics. On September 20, 1565, when Menéndez and 400 of his men arrived at the mouth of the St. Johns River, Jean Ribault, the Huguenot leader, decided to wage an attack by sea. Before he could carry it out, a small storm turned into a hurricane, wrecking the Huguenots' ships. Ribault had left the fort unmanned, so Menéndez was able to travel overland and wage a surprise attack on the Frenchmen, who lost 140 men. Menéndez told his men to spare only those who were either musicians or professing Catholics. Not one Spaniard was slain. After capturing Fort Caroline, which had been named for King Charles IX of France, Menéndez changed its name to San Mateo.

CHRISTMAS

Christmas was first celebrated on the North American continent in 1539 by a Spanish expedition led by Hernando de Soto. It was a mass presided over by some of the 12 Catholic priests on the expedition.

The mass was held in the Indian village of Anhayea, where de Soto and his men spent the fall and winter of 1539–40. Here they established a chain of forts and missions, with the purpose of converting the Apalache Indians to Christianity.

In 1824, the site was selected as the capital of the Territory of Florida. The small hill where the mass was held is now in Tallahassee, less than half a mile from the state capitol building.

From Seaplanes to Spaceships

SCHEDULED PASSENGER AIRLINE

Today three bridges span Tampa Bay to connect St. Petersburg and Tampa, but in 1913 the only links between the two cities were a 12-hour train ride and a 3-hour boat trip. The St. Petersburg–Tampa Airboat Line, the world's first regularly scheduled passenger airline, would soon shorten the trip to 18 minutes.

At that time, St. Petersburg was a growing tourist town of about 9,000 people. Winter visitors came for a season that lasted from November until April. But few came by auto; the typical way to get to the Gulf Coast city was to take a train to Tampa, then catch one of the three steamers that made daily trips across the bay.

Flying Boat

When P. E. Fansler, an electrical engineer, read about aviation pioneer Tony Jannus's trip in a "flying boat" down the Mississippi River from Omaha to New Orleans, he had a revolutionary idea. What about a flying boat to connect St. Petersburg and Tampa? Fansler's idea was not to use a plane for occasional trips, but to have a scheduled airline, "running from somewhere to somewhere else," as he put it.

Tony Jannus's flight had been made in a biplane built by Thomas Wesley Benoist, a wealthy manufacturer of self-starters

Tony Jannus takes off in his "flying boat" on the first scheduled passenger airline flight, 1914. *Courtesy of the Florida State Archives*

for automobiles who had recently gone into the airplane-manufacturing business in St. Louis, Missouri. Fansler wrote to Benoist with his idea, and after a brief correspondence, the manufacturer became enthusiastic. He said he would build and furnish two planes if Fansler would establish a route and handle the business end.

Fansler readily agreed and immediately set out to secure funding for the project. He found an enthusiastic backer in L. A. Whitney, secretary of the St. Petersburg Chamber of Commerce. Enchanted with the idea of helping to write history, Whitney assisted with the fund-raising and put up $1,500 of his own money. He remained so pleased with his role in the project that his last wish, which was later carried out by his widow, was that his body be cremated and his ashes scattered from an airplane that followed the route of the first historic flight over Tampa Bay.

First Airline Contract

On December 17, 1913, 10 years to the day after man's first powered flight, Benoist signed the country's first airline contract, made with the City of St.

Petersburg. To launch the new venture, Benoist built a 1,250-pound plane and shipped it by rail from Paducah, Kentucky, to St. Petersburg. With a wingspan of 44 feet, it was 26 feet long and had a top speed of 64 miles per hour. Its Roberts 75-horsepower, two-cycle engine was capable of turning the propeller 600 revolutions per minute.

The contract called for the airline to provide two 18-minute flights daily over Tampa Bay from January 1 to March 31, 1914, with Tony Jannus as pilot. This was timed just right for the winter influx of tourists.

On New Year's Day 1914, after a downtown parade in St. Petersburg and a colorful ceremony before 3,000 onlookers, the first rides in the new plane were auctioned off, some for as much as $400. During the first flight, Jannus had to land the plane on water once due to engine trouble, but 23 minutes after leaving St. Petersburg he arrived in Tampa, where he was greeted by another enthusiastic crowd. The next day the *New York Times* carried the story on its front page.

Risky Business

Despite the fact that flying was still considered risky, hundreds of passengers gladly paid the five-dollar, one-way fare for the 23-mile trip. By the time the three-month contract ended, the airline had carried 1,204 passengers.

The airline had been a success, but its contract was not renewed. The costs of equipment and mechanical devices were higher than expected.

FIRST AIR FREIGHT

On January 13, 1914, the St. Petersburg–Tampa Airboat Line carried the world's first shipment of air freight—50 pounds of ham and bacon from Swift and Company in Tampa to the Hefner Grocery Company in St. Petersburg.

THEY LAUGHED

After the first flight of the St. Petersburg–Tampa Airboat Line, the *Jacksonville News* printed this comment: "St. Petersburg papers might secure an obituary sketch of all aeroplane passengers at the same time they take the passenger manifests. It might save time." The sarcasm was unwarranted. Although the plane was forced down twice by engine trouble, the short-lived airline maintained a perfect safety record.

War in Europe was threatening America, and money was tight. The original backers withdrew their financial support. Although the airboat line was discontinued, it brought worldwide publicity to St. Petersburg and helped establish it as a popular winter vacation spot.

Two years later, Jannus was killed in an air accident while training Russian pilots, and Benoist died soon afterward in a streetcar accident.

PERMANENT PASSENGER AIRLINE

While large commercial airlines have come and gone since the early days of aviation, tiny Chalk's International Airlines has been flying between Miami and the Bahama Islands since 1919. It was the world's first permanent airline with regularly scheduled passenger service.

The Red Arrow Flying Service, as it was originally called, actually started transporting passengers from Miami to Bimini two years earlier. A. B. "Pappy" Chalks began operations from the docks of the Royal Palm Hotel with one three-seat seaplane, a Stinson Voyager. World War I intervened, however, and the Kentucky native enlisted as a Marine aviator. After the war, he returned to Miami and reestablished his business as Chalk's International Airlines.

Chalk's International Airlines sent seaplanes to the Bahamas from its Watson Island headquarters in the 1930s. *Courtesy of the Florida State Archives*

Prohibition and Rumrunning

By a quirk of fate, business boomed. Prohibition was in effect, and rum-running, the smuggling of liquor into the United States from the Bahamas, was a bustling and lucrative enterprise. The liquor was brought by boat to Miami, where it was distributed throughout the eastern states. The smugglers, however, preferred to fly and often booked passage on the new airline. So did the lawmen chasing them.

In 1926, Chalks's success enabled him to build a terminal on a newly created landfill named Watson Island, across from downtown Miami. It has been the airline's main operating base ever since.

The repeal of Prohibition in 1933 brought an end to rumrunning, but by then Chalk's was well established. Miami had become a mecca for winter tourists, many of whom wanted to extend their visit to the Bahamas. Pappy Chalks continued to pilot for the company until 1966, logging almost 17,000 hours. He died in 1977, at the age of 88.

The Chalk's fleet has grown to include five Grumman Turbine Mallards, each seating 17 passengers. The picturesque seaplanes have become a symbol of Miami and still splash down daily beside the world's busiest cruise ship port in the heart of the city.

☀ To Visit: Chalk's International Airlines

Chalk's International Airlines
1000 MacArthur Causeway
Miami, FL 33312
800-4CHALKS (for reservations and information)

A COLORFUL HISTORY

★ Chalk's International Airlines claims to be the most photographed airline in the world. No other can boast as colorful a history. Among the famous and infamous on the passenger lists have been Errol Flynn, Judy Garland, Lana Turner, Howard Hughes, Al Capone, Julio Iglesias, Jimmy Buffett, and Don Johnson.

★ In 1933, when deposed Cuban dictator Gerardo Machado was forced to flee his country by boat, Pappy Chalks picked him up in Nassau and flew him to exile in Miami. And Ernest Hemingway became a regular passenger when he discovered that Bimini had some of the best big-game fishing in the world.

★ Chalk's is probably the only airline where passengers complain the flights are not long enough. They are often more excited about the water take-offs and splashdowns than they are about their vacation destinations.

NAVAL AIR STATION

Situated on a bluff first explored by Spanish settlers in the 16th century, the Naval Air Station Pensacola is almost as old as aviation itself. In fact, the Wright brothers, well known for making the first successful powered airplane flight, were among those who worked to persuade the secretary of the navy that the new flying machine would be a welcome addition to the United States Navy.

Thus began a series of tests, the most convincing of which were performed by civilian pilot Eugene Ely. On November 14, 1910, Ely launched his 50-horsepower Curtiss plane from a wooden platform on the cruiser *Birmingham,* anchored at Hampton Roads, Virginia. Ely received a letter from Secretary of the Navy George von L. Meyer with congratulations for being "the first aviator in the world to have accomplished this feat." On January 18, 1911, Ely successfully landed on the deck of the armored cruiser USS *Pennsylvania* in San Francisco Bay and later took off from there.

Early planes at the Pensacola Naval Aeronautic Station, now called the Naval Air Station Pensacola. *Courtesy of the University of South Florida*

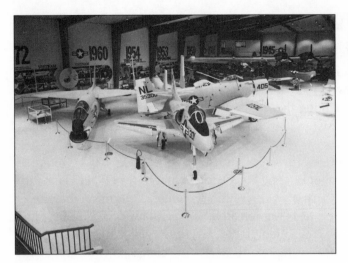

U.S. Navy airplanes are on display at the National Museum of Naval Aviation. *Courtesy of the Florida State Archives*

Proud of his accomplishment, he wrote to his supervisor: "I have proved that a machine can leave a ship and return to it, and others have proved that an aeroplane can remain in the air for a long time, so I guess the value of the aeroplane for the navy is unquestioned."

More Tests

The Navy Department agreed and the same year persuaded Congress to allocate $25,000 to the Bureau of Navigation for more experiments and tests to determine if the U.S. Navy should indeed become airborne. The first naval flight organization began operations at a camp near Annapolis, Maryland. The experiments were considered a success, and in 1913, Secretary of the Navy Josephus Daniels recommended to the navy's General Board that an aviation training station be established on the site of an abandoned navy yard in Pensacola, Florida. The board agreed that Pensacola's year-round flying weather and landlocked bay, along with facilities in the old navy yard that could easily be converted for other uses, made the site the logical choice. The recommendation was approved, and the first U.S. naval air station was created in 1914. All navy pilots—9 officers and 23 mechanics—were ordered to report to the Pensacola Naval Aeronautic Station for duty.

By today's standards, life for the early student pilots was unbelievably primitive. Hangars were tents set up along the beach, with wooden ramps leading to the water. Pilots needed to learn how to glide the airplane, as motors often quit in midair. Instruments didn't exist, and training had to be done on the ground; the rudimentary wood-and-wire, open-air planes couldn't hold both an instructor and a student pilot.

At the beginning of World War I, Pensacola was the nation's only naval air station. It had 38 naval aviators, 163 enlisted men, and 54 airplanes. By the war's end in 1918, the Pensacola Naval Aeronautic Station had expanded to 438 officers and 5,538 enlisted men. Steel and wooden hangars now stretched a mile down the beach and housed seaplanes, dirigibles, and free kite balloons.

The Pensacola Naval Aeronautic Station later became the Naval Air Station Pensacola. Fifteen thousand aviation personnel were trained there in 1999. Its graduates have served in both world wars, as well as in the Korean, Vietnam, and Desert Storm conflicts. Many famous astronauts, including Wally Schirra, Alan Shepard, Scott Carpenter, and John Glenn, also received their training at NAS Pensacola.

☼ To Visit: Naval Air Station Pensacola/National Museum of Naval Aviation

Visitors can take a self-guided tour, which includes the museum.

Naval Air Station Pensacola
1750 Radford Boulevard
Pensacola, FL 32508
850-623-7331

National Museum of Naval Aviation

The National Museum of Naval Aviation has the largest, most comprehensive display of naval flying equipment in the world. It contains a specimen of every U.S. Navy plane ever flown.

National Museum of Naval Aviation
3455 Taylor Road (on the grounds of the naval air station)
Pensacola, FL 32508
850-452-3604
Hours: Daily, 9 A.M.-5 P.M.
Closed Thanksgiving, Christmas, and New Year's Day.
Admission free; charge for IMAX theater and flight simulator.

BLUE ANGELS

The Naval Air Station Pensacola is home to the world-famous exhibition team the Blue Angels.

AIRSHIP ORDINANCE

In 1908, Kissimmee, now a major traffic artery for visitors to the world-famous Walt Disney World Resort, was a small cow town. To this day, no one knows why mayor T. M. Murphy and city attorney P. A. Vans Agnew got together to pass a law that would restrict flights over the town. Old-timers later remembered it as a joke, and that seems to be a logical explanation. At the time, five years after Orville Wright's first flight at Kitty Hawk, no airplane had ever flown anywhere over Florida. Only a dozen or so people had ever flown in any kind of motorized aircraft anywhere in the world.

Still, the headlines of the July 17, 1908, *Kissimmee Valley Gazette* read "AIRSHIP ORDINANCE SUGGESTED." It was proposed that regulations apply to any "flying machine or airship" traveling anywhere from 10 feet to 20 miles above the town. The proposed ordinance gave specifications for brakes, lights, and signal systems.

Stiff Fees

All aircraft would have to be licensed, with helicopters charged $150 per year and airplanes $100. Aircraft would be breaking the law if they dropped anything or collided with telephone poles or public buildings. The penalty: "Five hundred dollars or . . . imprisonment in the town calaboose for not more than 90 days."

Mayor Murphy, at first ridiculed and nearly laughed out of town, was soon hailed as a man with an uncanny vision of the future. In newspapers throughout the United States, Kissimmee was cited as a "progressive and farsighted little city." London, Paris, Berlin, and Amsterdam were among the cities that modeled airspace regulations after Kissimmee's ordinance, and the U.S. War Department wrote for a copy.

Despite all the hoopla and acclaim, the city council never passed the law. Yet as a model ordinance for cities all over the world, it gave Kissimmee the distinction of being the birthplace of aviation legislation.

MORE FIRSTS IN AERONAUTICS

Since the early days of aviation, Florida, with its mild climate, flat landscape, and proximity to Latin America, has been a hub of aeronautical activity. Some other firsts:

1911

★ **Air/sea rescue**—The first air/sea rescue was made on January 30, 1911, when Jack Douglas McCurdy was forced to ditch his plane in the sea because of a broken oil line. McCurdy was attempting to make the first flight from Key West to Cuba. He was picked up by his escort ship, the USS *Parlding*.

★ **Wireless message from air to ground**—Later in 1911, flying in a Curtiss biplane over Palm Beach, McCurdy sent a wireless message from the air to the ground and received an answer. It was the first time this had been done, and two weeks before it was demonstrated in a formal exhibition on Long Island, New York.

★ **West-to-east transcontinental flight**—Robert G. Fowler piloted the first west-to-east transcontinental airplane flight from Pasadena, California, to Jacksonville in 1911. The trip took 115 days.

★ **Night flight**—Lincoln Beachey, who in 1910 had been the first person to pilot an airplane in Florida, made the world's first night flight, over Tampa, a year later.

1915

★ **Service school of aerial photography**—The first service school of aerial photography opened at Pensacola Naval Aeronautic Station (now Naval Air Station Pensacola) in 1915.

★ **Catapult launching from moving vessel**—The naval air station's first commanding officer, Lieutenant Commander Henry Mustin, made the first catapult launching of an aircraft from a moving vessel, the USS *North Carolina*, in Pensacola Bay in 1915.

1917

★ **Marine aviation force**—At Curtiss Field, which later became the Miami Springs Golf Course, more than 1,000 men were trained in the nation's first Marine aviation force in 1917.

1922

★ **Transcontinental flight in less than 24 hours**—On September 4, 1922, Lieutenant James H. "Jimmy" Doolittle piloted the first transcontinental flight made in less than a day from Pablo Beach (now Jacksonville Beach) to San Diego, California. Flying the 2,163 miles at a speed higher than 100 miles per hour, Doolittle made the trip in 21 hours and 20 minutes. The purpose of the flight was to prove to Congress the practicality of aviation for the military.

1927

★ **Female pilot to attempt transatlantic flight**—Twenty-year-old Ruth Elder, from Lakeland, was the first woman to attempt a flight across the Atlantic Ocean. On October 11, 1927, as co-pilot for her flight instructor, George Haldeman, she took off in the *American Girl,* a Stinson monoplane, from Long Island's Roosevelt Field, bound for Paris. Although an oil leak forced the two to ditch the plane before it reached its destination, the *American Girl* set an overwater record of 2,623 miles.

★ **Scheduled international flights**—In 1927, Miami-based Pan American Airways made the first regularly scheduled international flight by a United States airline. Departing from Key West, the Fokker F-7 trimotor airplane carried 28 sacks of mail and took 1 hour and 21 minutes to reach Havana, Cuba. Three months later, Pan American made the first scheduled passenger flight to Cuba. Because of Prohibition, the plane had to be christened with champagne in Havana, rather than in Key West, on its maiden voyage.

1929

★ **Scheduled flights to South America**—Pan American Airways made the first scheduled mail flight to South America (Miami to Cartagena, Colombia) in 1929. A few months after the mail flight, Pan American made the first scheduled passenger flight to South America, from Miami to Curaçao.

1932

★ **New York–to-Miami flight**—Miami-based Eastern Airlines made the first New York–to-Miami flight in 1932. The trip took 13 hours and 50 minutes.

1958

★ **Domestic jet airline service**—In 1958, Miami-based National Airlines introduced domestic jet airline service in the United States with a route from Miami to New York.

FIRSTS IN SPACE

The United States space program wins hands down as Florida's most famous and most ambitious first. Indeed, it is the most ambitious project

The John F. Kennedy Space Center launches *Discovery. Courtesy of the John F. Kennedy Space Center*

The *Challenger* mission STS-8 was the first night launch of the space shuttle. *Courtesy of the John F. Kennedy Space Center*

ever devised by man. But as with many great things, its beginnings were small; and its initial endeavor was a failure. Mercer Livermore King, a reporter who covered the first aborted attempt to launch a rocket, *Bumper* 7, into outer space on July 19, 1950, described it this way: "There was nothing out there but palmetto scrub and rattlesnakes. It was too hot for mosquitoes." Another Florida paper reported: "When they finally got around to pulling the firing switch . . . it produced only a popping noise, hardly worthy of a champagne cork." The launching was scrubbed, and rescheduled for five days later.

Through the years, there have been many more failures and disappointments, and even a few tragedies. But from that small beginning, man has gone on to orbit the earth, walk on the moon, send satellites to other planets, and build orbiting stations to live and work in space. Today, the John F. Kennedy Space Center covers 110,000 acres on Cape Canaveral. Thousands of scientists, engineers, and technicians work with enormous rockets and sophisticated spacecraft in the complex of computer-run control centers and towering launch pads.

The tallest part of the Vehicle Assembly Building has four bays to assemble space shuttles and ready them for flight. *Courtesy of the John F. Kennedy Space Center*

To describe all of the firsts of the United States space program would take volumes. Here are a few of the highlights:

★ **Successful rocket launching**—At 9:29 A.M. on July 24, 1950, a makeshift rocket on a crude launch pad blasted off from Cape Canaveral. Control centers were located in trenches, a tent, and an old army tank. From the sandy road leading to the launch site, snakes and alligators watched with the 30-man launch team as *Bumper 7* zoomed 10 miles into the air. A few minutes later it dropped 50 miles away, into the Atlantic Ocean.

★ **Rocket to orbit the earth**—On January 31, 1958, *Explorer I* was blasted from its launch pad and into an orbit of the earth. Two years later, *Tiros I* became the first weather satellite to orbit the earth.

★ **American in space**—In 1961, the U.S. space program was lagging behind that of the Soviet Union. On April 12, Soviet astronaut Yuri Gagarin had not only already penetrated the barrier of space but had actually orbited the earth. Manned flight did not become a reality in the United States until May 5, 1961, when Alan B. Shepard Jr. blasted off in a Mercury-Redstone rocket, *Freedom 7*, to become the first American in space. In a 15-minute ride, he ascended 115 nautical miles, covering a 302-mile range. Russian premier Nikita Khrushchev's declaration that Shepard's trip was a "flea jump" prompted President John F. Kennedy to plead before a joint session of Congress on May 25, 1961, to step up the effort to put the United States first in the space race. "I believe," he said, "that this nation should commit itself to achieving the goal, before this decade is out, of landing a man on the moon and returning him safely to Earth."

★ **American to orbit the earth**—On February 20, 1962, astronaut John H. Glenn Jr., wearing a pressurized suit, almost filled the tiny capsule of Mercury *Friendship 7* as he prepared for the first American manned flight to orbit the earth. Traveling at 17,500 miles per hour, 160 miles above the earth, Glenn had to call on his extensive knowledge and training, as well as his personal courage, when the autopilot function failed and he was forced to pilot the craft manually. Mission Control received a signal that the heat shield, which would prevent the capsule from burning up during reentry, was loose. Glenn was ordered to retain his retropacket package, which normally would have been jettisoned after the rockets were fired, to hold the heat shield in place. Neither Glenn nor Mission Control could be sure this would work, but fortunately the heat shield held, and Glenn splashed down safely after orbiting the earth three times during the five-hour trip.

On October 29, 1998, Glenn scored another first when, at the age of 77, he became the first senior citizen in space, traveling aboard the space shuttle *Discovery*. The purpose of his mission was to study the parallels between space flight and the aging process.

★ **Man on the moon**—While the United States seemed to lag behind the Soviet Union in the space race through most of the 1960s, it soared ahead at the end of the decade when American astronauts took mankind's first walk on the moon.

An astronaut explores space independent of his command module. *Courtesy of the John F. Kennedy Space Center*

On July 16, 1969, astronauts Neil Armstrong, Edwin "Buzz" Aldrin, and Michael Collins lifted off in *Apollo 11*, a Saturn V rocket. Also aboard were the command module *Columbia*, a service module, and the lunar module *Eagle*. On July 19, *Apollo 11* orbited the moon. The next day, Armstrong and Aldrin descended to the surface in the lunar module, while Collins stayed in the orbiting spacecraft. Later that day, Armstrong walked down a ladder descended from the *Eagle* and touched the moon as he proclaimed: "One small step for man, one giant leap for mankind."

When the *Columbia,* carrying the three astronauts, splashed down southwest of Hawaii on July 24, it marked the fulfillment of President Kennedy's challenge to send a man to the moon and return him safely to earth before the end of the decade.

★ **Manned space station**—When *Skylab 1* was launched into space on May 14, 1973, it was the first manned orbital U.S. space station and the largest spacecraft ever built. Weighing more than 100 tons, it stretched 118 feet from end to end. It was as large as a three-bedroom house and had most of the same comforts. The three passengers had to share a shower and lavatory, but each had a private compartment for sleeping. Also aboard were scientific and medical equipment, 720 gallons of drinking water, and more than 2,000 tons of food. The purpose of *Skylab* was to see if man could live and work in space for the long periods of time it would take to travel back and forth to other planets and moons.

★ **Woman in space**—From June 18 to 24, 1983, Sally Ride, America's first woman in space, was mission specialist on the seventh flight of the space shuttle *Challenger*. She operated a robotic arm that deployed and retrieved satellites.

Some later women astronauts were Judith Resnik, mission specialist on the ill-fated *Challenger*; Shannon Lucid, American record-holder for the longest time spent in space; Eileen Collins, first female commander of a space flight; and Pam Melroy, pilot on the 100th shuttle launch.

★ **Untethered spacewalk**—On February 3, 1984, astronauts Bruce McCandless and Robert Stewart left the shuttle *Challenger* to walk in space, using only a large, nitrogen-propelled jetpack called the Manned Maneuvering unit. The astronauts ventured 300 feet away from the shuttle, then returned to the payload bay, controlling the unit by hand. It was America's first untethered walk in space. Since the jetpack was bulky and expensive, it was used on only five more missions and was later replaced by a smaller device known as the Simplified Aid for EVA Rescue.

★ **Civilian in space**—When the time came for the first civilian to be launched into space, it seemed fitting that it should be a teacher. Christa McAuliffe, a New Hampshire high school teacher and mother of two, was chosen to go along on the shuttle *Challenger.* The purpose of her ride was to show that space travel is safe for civilians.

It was January 28, 1986, and the temperature was in the 20s. As the shuttle lifted off, thousands watched on television and many more watched from the ground. One minute and 13 seconds after liftoff, a stunned nation saw the *Challenger*'s huge external fuel tank blow apart, destroying the shuttle in midair. Christa McAuliffe and six other crew members died.

Due to the sub-freezing temperatures, a seal on one of the shuttle's solid rocket boosters had failed. Flames escaped and burned through the fuel tank, causing the explosion. After the accident, NASA changed nearly all aspects of its shuttle fleet. It would be more than two years before the next mission would fly.

 ## To Visit: John F. Kennedy Space Center/U.S. Astronaut Hall of Fame

The John F. Kennedy Space Center complex is on Merritt Island, 6 miles east of U.S. Highway 1 on State Road 405.

John F. Kennedy Space Center Visitors' Complex
321-867-5000
Hours: Daily, 9 A.M.-dusk
Closed Christmas Day.
Admission charged.

U.S. Astronaut Hall of Fame
The U.S. Astronaut Hall of Fame, directly across the Indian River from the space center, has interactive exhibits such as a flight simulator and a G-force trainer with four times the pull of gravity. A theater in a full-size replica of a space shuttle offers multimedia presentations.

U.S. Astronaut Hall of Fame
6225 Vectorspace Boulevard
Titusville, FL 32780
321-269-6100
Hours: Daily, 9 A.M.-5 P.M.
Admission charged.

Builders, Visionaries, and Heroes

CHAPTER

3

LARGE BUILDING OF POURED CONCRETE

Eighty years before Walt Disney built his Magic Kingdom for the masses in Orlando, Henry Flagler built a fantasy castle for the rich in St. Augustine. By bringing his railroad to the old city, Flagler had made St. Augustine accessible to wealthy winter tourists, who of course wanted the finest in accommodations. Flagler obliged with his magnificent Hotel Ponce de Leon, the first large building in the nation to be constructed of poured concrete.

The idea of pouring liquid concrete into wooden forms and casting it into a single, seamless monolith came from Franklin W. Smith, a Boston philanthropist and amateur architect who had used the process in building his St. Augustine residence. Portland cement, a relatively new invention, provided a binder for the concrete strong enough to enable it to be used in large buildings. For an aggregate, Flagler added coquina shell and sand, which barges brought to the hotel site from offshore islands.

Fantasyland

In order for the new hotel to harmonize with the city's Spanish-style buildings, Flagler sent an architect to Spain to gather ideas. When the architect returned, he proposed that the hotel be built in the style of a Moorish palace. Flagler liked the idea and spared no

At the turn of the 20th century, the Hotel Ponce de Leon was a majestic sight. *Courtesy of the Florida State Archives*

expense in creating a Spanish-Mediterranean fantasyland. The Ponce de Leon covered 4½ acres and had the most modern kitchen facilities, two water towers, writing and smoking rooms, a barber shop, a ladies' billiard room, and electric power throughout. Two Castilian towers dominated the huge structure. Acres of beautifully tended gardens interspersed with Moorish cloisters and Gothic niches grew behind a medieval portcullis. In the lobby were a nine-foot grand piano, coats of arms of noble Spanish families, and treasures of marble, onyx, and silver.

In the dining hall, guests could enjoy dinner under a barrel-vaulted ceiling with orchestra balconies at either end. Each table had four matching carved-oak chairs, imported from Austria, and its own Oriental rug. Bedrooms were heated by steam, a rarity at the time, but each also had a magnificent fireplace.

The Ponce de Leon opened for its first winter season in January 1888. The first grand ball was held in the dining hall, with an orchestra playing in each balcony. Among the guests were Mrs. Ulysses S. Grant and Frederick Vanderbilt. A month after the opening, President Grover Cleveland visited the hotel driven in a coach drawn by four white horses.

WHITE ELEPHANT

Eighty years after the Ponce de Leon was built, wealthy winter tourists had abandoned St. Augustine for Palm Beach and Miami. There was no demand for a luxury hotel. The Ponce de Leon, built to last for centuries, could not be demolished and became an enormous white elephant. Today it is the home of Flagler College.

Other presidents, foreign dignitaries, and the elite of the day were frequent guests. For five decades, the Ponce de Leon was reputedly the most exclusive winter resort in the nation.

Amidst all the splendor, however, Flagler neglected a much-needed amenity. Guests had to go down the hall to community bathrooms. As they began to demand private baths in rooms for which they were paying up to $75 a day, Flagler was forced to add them later.

WORLD WAR II HERO

In 1942, at the young age of 23, Alexander "Sandy" R. Nininger died a hero. He was the first American soldier in World War II to be awarded the Congressional Medal of Honor.

Nininger, a Fort Lauderdale resident and West Point graduate, served in the 57th Infantry of the Philippine Scouts. As the Japanese progressed in their initial attacks, which would ultimately result in the infamous Bataan Death March, Nininger organized a patrol to gather information on the Japanese forces. During this patrol, the Japanese savagely attacked the Americans and their Filipino defenders and began to overrun Nininger's position. His memorial plaque describes the battle:

> Single-handedly, Sandy Nininger . . . charged into the enemy
> positions with a rifle, grenades, and fixed bayonet. Shooting

Sandy R. Nininger posthumously received the first Congressional Medal of Honor in World War II. *Courtesy of the Florida State Archives*

snipers out of trees and destroying enemy groups in fox holes, he plunged forward. Then, seizing a Japanese machine gun, he continued onward, killing at least forty enemy and forcing many others to retreat.

Victory

Still clutching the enemy's machine gun, Nininger was mortally wounded. Inspired by his bravery, his fellow soldiers counterattacked and won the battle. General Douglas MacArthur said it was this victory that gave the Americans time to prepare Manila and Corregidor for the defense. For his heroism, Nininger was posthumously awarded the first Congressional Medal of Honor in World War II by President Franklin D. Roosevelt.

NAVY SEALS

The Navy SEAL (for *sea, air,* and *land*) teams, the most elite and highly trained group in the U.S. armed forces, were first trained at the United States Naval Training Base in Fort Pierce, Florida. Then known as Naval Combat Demolition Units (NCDUs), the first class graduated in 1943 and was immediately sent to Europe to clear the way for American troops to land in Sicily.

The SEALs, who work in teams of up to 16 men, have scored remarkable successes and become legendary for their exploits. They often perform clandestine operations and engage in counter-guerrilla warfare. It takes nerves of steel and a special kind of patriotism, as well as supreme physical and mental capabilities, to be able to do this kind of work. Recruits must show that they are highly motivated and will complete their mission to the best of their ability, regardless of the hazards or the effort involved. In one of their early tasks, Operation Overlord in the World War II landing of U.S. troops in Normandy, nearly 40 percent of the NCDUs became casualties. Still, the operation was considered a success and paved the way for the end of the war in Europe. The NCDUs were then sent to the Pacific to continue their work of beach reconnaissance and clearing. From Borneo to Saipan to Okinawa, they were credited with saving thousands of lives.

During the Korean War, in addition to clearing harbors and beaches, Underwater Demolition Teams (UDTs) were given the task of demolishing inland railroads, bridges, and tunnels. It was largely through their work that the United Nations forces were able to stage a massive landing and change the course of the war.

In 1962, the UDTs formed units called SEAL teams and were sent to Vietnam. Here they performed their most heroic and legendary exploits. Several books have been written about this period in the history of the SEALs.

MAN TO BREAK SOUND BARRIER IN FREE FALL

On August 16, 1960, when Orlando native Joe W. Kittinger Jr. broke the sound barrier, the feat had been accomplished many times before. It was the way he did it that made history.

Could the sound barrier be broken by just the speed of a falling human body? It seemed impossible. But *impossible* was obviously not in Kittinger's vocabulary. If it had been, he never would have stepped out of the gondola of a helium balloon at an altitude of 102,800 feet to fall to the earth. This set a world record for a parachute jump, but what happened next is even more astounding. Kittinger had no means of protection other than "a space suit, a parachute, and guts," as a newspaper article later described it. He fell for four minutes before his main chute opened. In the vacuum of the upper stratosphere, the speed of his falling body reached 714 miles per hour, breaking the sound barrier.

Not a Stunt

Kittinger was a colonel in the U.S. Air Force, and this was no daredevil stunt. His work was a vital part of research conducted by the air force to determine the feasibility of sending human beings into space. He had already made two jumps from more than 70,000 feet and two trips to the stratosphere in prototypes of the first space capsules. His mission this time was to determine whether an astronaut could work outside of his command module in the vacuum of space and whether he could possibly return to earth without it, should that become necessary. "When I made that jump 38 years ago," he recalled in 1998, "it wasn't done to set a record. It was done to gather information for the space program and the United States Air Force. We had never exposed a man in a space environment, but we knew one day he would need to get out of his craft and work out there."

TRANSATLANTIC BALLOON FLIGHT

On a flight that began on September 14, 1984, Colonel Joe W. Kittinger Jr. became the first person to cross the Atlantic Ocean solo in a balloon. The trip lasted four days.

A Hero

Kittinger later served three combat tours in Vietnam, and was shot down near Hanoi and held as a prisoner of war for over a year. He has logged over 15,000 hours of flight time in 68 different types of aircraft.

He was recently enshrined in the National Aviation Hall of Fame and named an Elder Statesman of Aviation by the National Aeronautic Association (NAA). He is the subject of a Naval Institute book, *The Pre-Astronauts*, by Craig Ryan.

BLACK WOMAN TO HEAD A FEDERAL AGENCY

After serving as President Franklin D. Roosevelt's special adviser on minority affairs from 1935 to 1944, Mary McLeod Bethune was appointed director of the Division of Negro Affairs of the National Youth Administration. She was the first black woman to head a federal agency.

This was the latest in a long line of accomplishments for this remarkable woman. Born in 1875 in Mayesville, South Carolina, she was one of 17 children of Samuel and Patsy McLeod, who had been freed from slavery only a decade before her birth. With no money but an unshakable faith in God and a firm belief that nothing is impossible, she determined early in life to pave the way for those of her race to achieve greatness.

Mary McLeod Bethune was appointed head of a federal agency by President Franklin D. Roosevelt. *Courtesy of the Florida State Archives*

The Key to Success

Mary McLeod was convinced that education was the key to success, and that she would have to start with an education for herself. It seemed an impossible goal for an illiterate black girl working in the cotton fields, but she turned to God for help. Her prayers were answered when a Presbyterian mission teacher came to her county and invited her to become a pupil in the teacher's school. Mary gladly walked 10 miles every day to attend, and later received scholarships to Scotia Seminary and the Moody Bible Institute in Chicago.

In 1904, with only $1.50, she founded the Daytona Normal and Industrial Institute for Negro Girls in Daytona Beach. The site was a former trash dump with an old, run-down house, for which she talked the owner into taking a $5 down payment and $5 a month when she could get it. "We burned logs and used the charred splinters as pencils and mashed elderberries for ink," she later recalled of the school's early days. In 1923, it became Bethune-Cookman College, one of the country's leading colleges for African American students. In honor of the prayers that made it all possible, Bethune named the first large building Faith Hall.

National Honors

Due to her outstanding work in education and her fight against racial injustice throughout the country, Bethune became involved in many activities on a national scale. She served as president of the National Association of Colored Women and vice president of the National Association for the Advancement of Colored People (NAACP). She was appointed consultant on interracial affairs at the charter conference of the United Nations. Presidents from Calvin Coolidge to Harry Truman named her to government posts. She died on May 18, 1955.

HONORED

When Mary McLeod Bethune received an honorary degree from Rollins College in 1949, she was the first black woman to be so honored by a white southern college.

It was a sultry June day in 1849 when Dr. John Gorrie announced to his friend and colleague Dr. Alvan Wentworth Chapman that he had found a way to make ice. He had, in fact, already produced several cubes the size of bricks—in Florida and in the summertime.

Chapman knew that his friend had been trying to find a cure for the dreaded yellow fever that had become epidemic in northwest Florida, particularly in their town of Apalachicola. Gorrie reasoned that since the fever thrived only in hot, moist climates, he could speed his patients' recovery by cooling their rooms. In 1844 he had built a machine to do just that.

A Fortunate Accident

Gorrie needed ice for his room-cooling project, and the only way he could get it was from ships that delivered it from northern waters. He suspended

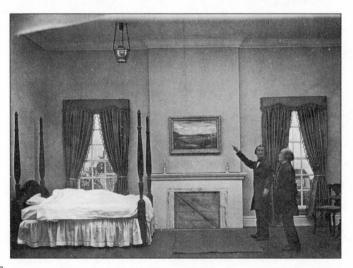

A statue at the John Gorrie State Museum depicts Gorrie pointing to his ice machine. *Courtesy of the Florida State Archives*

a basin of this ice from a hospital room ceiling and, with the help of two steam compressor pumps and a series of pipes, pulled warm air out of the room and sent cool air into it. In 1845, an attendant accidentally left the engine of the compressor pumps on overnight. The next morning, Gorrie found the pipes clogged with ice. Excitedly, he began designing his ice machine.

When Monsieur Rosan, a wealthy cotton trader and native of France, learned of the new machine, he asked Gorrie if he could provide the ice for a Bastille Day party at the Mansion House, at that time the largest hotel in Florida. The ice ship was late, and Rosan was not sure if he could cool his champagne. Gorrie assured him that not only could he produce the ice, he would do it in the same room where the party was to be held. When the ship failed to arrive, the Frenchman bet one of his friends a basket of champagne that he could provide artificial ice in time. Early on the day of the party, Gorrie set up his ice machine behind a screen in the room. That evening, as guests were arriving, he stepped from behind the screen with a dripping, brick-sized block of ice and placed it in Rosan's hand. When Rosan was presented with a bottle of champagne in front of his amazed guests, he uncorked it right away in celebration of Gorrie's accomplishment.

Gorrie was mistaken about cool air being a cure for yellow fever—no one had yet identified the lowly mosquito as the culprit—but his break-through did more than keep his patients more comfortable. It led to refrig-eration, which eliminated the need for the salting, pickling, and drying of food. It also led to air conditioning, which ultimately helped pave the way for Florida to rise out of obscurity and become the fourth-largest state, although that was not what Gorrie had had in mind for it. It was to be almost 80 years before the world would benefit from his inventions.

Hard Times

Despite Gorrie's genius as an inventor, he was not a particularly good businessman. He found a wealthy backer for his work, but the man died

A PROPHECY FULFILLED

While working to perfect his ice machine, Dr. John Gorrie made a prophetic statement: "We know of no want of mankind more urgent than a cheap means of producing artificial cold. The discovery would alter and extend the face of civilization."

before he could help, and Gorrie couldn't find another. He was granted patents for his ice machine in Washington and London in 1851, but they expired 20 years later due to lack of production. The powerful northern ice monopoly, fearful that Gorrie's invention would halt the lucrative business of shipping ice from frozen lakes and rivers, succeeded in enlisting the press to discredit him through a campaign of ridicule. One New York writer scoffed, "There is a crank down in Apalachicola, Florida, a Dr. John Gorrie, who claims he can make ice as good as God Almighty." Wounded by these attacks, Gorrie became discouraged, then gravely ill. He died on June 22, 1855.

In the years after Gorrie's death, others were credited with developing the ice machine and the air conditioner. Fortunately, Dr. Alvan Chapman lived until 1899 and talked to scientists from all over the world about his friend's inventions. Today John Gorrie is regarded as one of America's great inventors, and his statue is in the National Statuary Hall in Washington, D.C., where he represents Florida as one of her most outstanding citizens.

 To Visit: John Gorrie State Museum

A replica of the first ice machine, built from specifications of Gorrie's 1851 patent, is on display in the museum.

John Gorrie State Museum
Avenue D at Sixth Street
Apalachicola, FL 32320
850-653-9347
Hours: Thursday-Monday, 9 A.M.-5 P.M.
Admission charged.

WOMAN TO FOUND A MAJOR U.S. CITY

Although she was a woman and not allowed to vote for the incorporation of the city in 1896, Julia Tuttle has often been called "the mother of Miami." It was her donation of more than 300 acres of land and her ability to persuade Henry Flagler to bring his railroad to the small trading post on the Miami River that spawned the birth of one of the nation's major cities.

With the immense wealth he had acquired as John D. Rockefeller's partner in Standard Oil, Flagler began developing the east coast of Florida in 1885, when he transformed sleepy St. Augustine into a prosperous winter resort by bringing his railroad to the town. Every few years he pushed the railroad farther south, paving the way for more development.

A Visionary

Julia Tuttle envisioned a great city on the spot that had become her home, a place of lush vegetation and pristine beauty, where the Miami River flowed into Biscayne Bay. But vision couldn't become reality until the area was accessible. At the time, the only way in was by sea. She told Flagler she would donate half of her 640 acres of property holdings to build a city if he would extend his railroad 65 miles south from West Palm Beach.

Although Flagler didn't deny the beauty of Tuttle's "Biscayne Bay Country," he found it to be hot, marshy, and infested with mosquitoes. He considered her offer, but ultimately rejected it. The area, he thought, had little potential for development. Tuttle refused to give up, but when the

Julia Tuttle has often been called "the mother of Miami." *Courtesy of the Florida State Archives*

winter of 1894–95 brought two disastrous cold spells to Florida, the worst in six decades, she knew it wouldn't be easy to persuade Flagler to reconsider.

Orange Blossoms

The first cold spell, on December 29, 1894, destroyed most of the citrus crop in the central part of the state. On February 7, 1895, just as new growth was beginning to appear and growers were confident the danger was over, the second cold snap hit. It not only killed what fruit was left but destroyed the trees as well. Tuttle would somehow have to convince Flagler that the Miami area was free from the killing frost.

Two days after the second cold wave, Flagler sent an employee, James E. Ingraham, to investigate the damage. While central Florida's orange groves had been destroyed, Ingraham found southern Florida's citrus trees blooming and vegetables still growing, untouched by frost. He gathered a bouquet of fresh orange blossoms, put them in damp cotton, and showed them to Tuttle, who asked him to take them to Flagler. When he saw the blossoms, Flagler agreed that Miami must indeed be frost-free.

A New City

Nevertheless, he had to see for himself. In late February 1895, he traveled to Miami to meet with Tuttle. He arrived by boat on a beautiful, clear day and by nightfall had made the decision to accept her offer. He would extend his railroad to Miami, build a resort hotel there, and develop a city.

It was Flagler's custom to ride each of his trains as it reached a new station, so on April 13, 1896, he was aboard the first train that arrived in

MAJOR EVENTS

The arrival of the railroad was the first of four major events that shaped Miami's history. The others were:

★ The great Florida land boom of the 1920s, when the population quadrupled in four years.

★ World War II, when thousands of military personnel trained in Miami and its suburbs. Many GIs returned after the war and became permanent residents.

★ The Cuban Revolution, which began when Fidel Castro came to power in 1959, sending hordes of Cubans to the area. Miami became a multicultural gateway to Latin America.

Miami to a crowd of delighted onlookers. Later that year, Miami was incorporated as a city.

NORTH-TO-SOUTH HIGHWAY

The Dixie Highway, the first highway to traverse the country from north to south, came about largely through the efforts of the builder of Miami Beach, Carl Fisher.

Fisher was a wealthy Midwestern industrialist who had made a name for himself as the inventor of the Prest-O-Lite auto lamp, which made night driving possible. He also built the Indianapolis Speedway and initiated a 500-mile auto race that he named the Indianapolis 500. He had already been instrumental in building one cross-country highway, the Lincoln Highway, from the west to the east.

In January 1912, Fisher took his pretty, young wife, Jane, to Miami for a vacation. Over Jane's protests, they crossed Biscayne Bay to a swampy, alligator-infested island. On the site of what is now Lincoln Road in Miami Beach, Fisher picked up a stick and drew plans in the sand for a great city. Later, by dredging sand from the bottom of the bay and filling in the swamps, he transformed the island into the wealthy resort city of Miami Beach.

New Highway Needed

After World War I, tourists with money to spend began coming to Miami Beach by rail and by automobile. Fisher had provided the financing for a wooden bridge to his new island city, but he still needed a highway for motorists from the North and the Midwest. He soon found, however, that support for this highway would be much more difficult to garner than it had been for the Lincoln Highway. Most southerners were still too poor to buy automobiles or build roads for them, so the automobile industry was less than enthusiastic about a north–south highway.

Once Fisher did gain government approval, however, he found both northern and southern states eager to contribute ideas of their own about the new highway. They all wanted the prestige of having the Dixie Highway run through their cities. Fisher lengthened his original proposal of a highway from Indianapolis to Miami to include both Sault Sainte Marie and Chicago. In April 1915, when the Chattanooga Automobile Club held a conference for governors and others interested in the project, 5,000 people attended. From this conference, the Dixie Highway Association was formed and modeled after the group that had successfully promoted the Lincoln Highway.

Controversy

The group seemed to divide into two warring factions. One side wanted the highway to follow the Atlantic coastline, while the other wanted it farther west. Fisher appeased both groups by adding a stretch of highway that would run through the eastern states. When completed, the Dixie Highway stretched nearly 4,000 miles, from Sault Sainte Marie to Miami.

In October 1915, Fisher arrived in Miami at the head of a Dixie Highway Pathfinders' Tour, an automobile procession that had begun in Chicago. Almost all Miami residents turned out for a festive reception. The new Dixie Highway, also known as U.S. Highway 1, ran right to Miami Beach, where motorists now could readily find Fisher's real estate office and hotels. And America had the beginnings of a mammoth system of highways that provided easy access anywhere in the nation.

SLAIN CIVIL RIGHTS LEADER

Harry T. Moore is almost unknown outside Florida, and for many years he was largely forgotten even in his home state. But despite the fact that he was not as well known as Eldredge Cleaver, Malcolm X, and Dr. Martin Luther King Jr., he was the first to die for their cause.

The home of Harry T. and Harriette Moore the day after it was bombed. *Courtesy of the Florida State Archives*

In 1951, years before Dr. King began his ministry, a handful of blacks dared to challenge the white man's assumption that it was their duty to "know their place." In 1951, that was an extremely dangerous thing to do. It was a time when blacks moved meekly to the back of the bus rather than risk legal consequences, when eyewitnesses to violent crimes by whites against blacks often conveniently forgot what they had seen when it came time to testify in court. It was a time before a tightly organized civil rights movement, when anyone who challenged the accepted way of doing things was mostly on his own.

A Challenger

Despite the danger, Moore, a black schoolteacher, overcame his shyness to become one of the most vocal and proactive challengers to the status quo. In 1934, he organized a local chapter of the NAACP. He fought for equal pay for black and white teachers. He demanded investigations of hate crimes against blacks. For 17 years he traveled around Florida, encouraging others of his race to register and vote. In the little hamlet of Mims, which was accustomed to a social order that included strict segregation, he was considered a troublemaker and the most hated man in town.

Christmas Day 1951 was Moore's 25th wedding anniversary. That evening, with his mother, his wife, Harriette, and Peaches, their 23-year-old daughter, he enjoyed a quiet celebration at home in Mims. His other daughter, Evangeline, was on her way home from Washington, D.C., where she worked for the U.S. Department of Labor.

At 10:20 P.M., after the Moores had gone to bed, a blast suddenly tore apart their small frame house, killing Harry. The blast was caused by a high-powered bomb, planted under the house only hours earlier. Harry's mother and daughter survived, but Harriette died of her injuries nine days later, the day after her husband's funeral.

Unsolved Crime

Although speculation was rife as to who had committed the crime, no one was ever charged. The reopening of the case in 1991 by Governor Lawton Chiles failed to bring a solution, but it did focus public attention on the Moores. In 1996, the new $18 million Brevard County Courthouse was named the Harry T. and Harriette V. Moore Justice Center and dedicated as a memorial to the slain couple.

BILLY GRAHAM SERMON

In the fall of 1934, after hearing a traveling evangelist in his hometown of Charlotte, North Carolina, 16-year-old Billy Graham made a personal commitment to Christ. In 1939, while still a student at the Florida Bible Institute in Temple Terrace, he realized his calling. He affirmed: "O God, if you want me to preach, I will do it."

MOST ADMIRED

Billy Graham has been listed by the Gallup Poll as one of the 10 most admired men in the world 42 times, more than any other person.

Graham wasted no time in preaching his first sermon. It was outside a saloon in Tampa's Franklin Street neighborhood, where he preached to derelicts and skid row bums. An irate bartender knocked him down and pushed his face into the ground. The fledgling evangelist picked himself up and went on to launch a spectacular career.

Message to the World

After graduating from the Florida Bible Institute in 1940, the Reverend Dr. Graham enrolled in Wheaton College in Illinois and graduated in 1943. His first big crusade was held in Los Angeles in 1949. His American crusades attracted crowds of thousands, and in 1957 a Madison Square Garden crusade lasted 16 weeks. Graham went on to launch these gatherings worldwide and to become the man who has preached to more people than any other person in history—over 210 million in more than 185 countries and territories. Hundreds of millions more followers have been reached through television. His audiences have been composed of people from every walk of life, from Australian bushmen to heads of state. He has counseled presidents and written 18 bestselling books.

In November 2000, amid rumors that age and ill health would force him to retire, Graham returned to Florida for a four-night crusade in Jacksonville. "I am looking forward to many more months and possibly years of crusade ministry," he said.

RANCHER TO DIP CATTLE

Dipping cattle in concrete vats containing a chemical solution to rid them of ticks is standard practice by cattlemen today. It was first done around 1912 by Bertha Palmer, a wealthy Chicago society matron–turned-Floridian.

Palmer, with her upswept hair, velvet choker, and pearl earrings, was a far cry from what one would expect a cattle baron to be. A society leader, she reigned not only in the Windy City but also in Paris, London, and Newport. As the wife of Potter Palmer, a prominent businessman and builder and owner of the exclusive Palmer House hotel, she frequently entertained American presidents and European royalty in her Gothic mansion on Chicago's Lake Shore Drive.

Bertha Palmer was a Chicago society leader before she became a pioneer cattle rancher in Sarasota. *Courtesy of the Florida State Archives*

A New Way of Life

The little fishing village of Sarasota, Florida, was an unlikely place for Palmer to choose as a new home. But after the death of her husband in 1902, she began to tire of the social scene. Long noted for her disdain of society phoniness and her refusal to fawn over royalty, she longed for a less complicated life.

In 1910, after reading an advertisement for Sarasota land in the *Chicago Tribune*, the 61-year-old dowager came to the little town of 900 residents in her private railroad car, along with her father and a staff of servants. "Here is heaven at last," she exclaimed when she saw Sarasota Bay. She purchased 1,300 acres of citrus groves, three ranches that included 3,000 head of cattle, and a home, which she named The Oaks and turned into a showplace. She bought land between Tampa and Venice that eventually totaled 140,000 acres. To the townspeople, who found her relaxed and easy to talk to, she brought jobs and, to some, prosperity.

Cattle Rancher

Far from the salons and drawing rooms of Chicago, Palmer became one of the nation's most successful cattle ranchers. She imported 17 Brahma bulls to breed with the scrawny Florida cows, descendants of those brought over by Spaniards two centuries earlier. But as she learned by doing, her mistakes brought snickers from the townspeople. She built silos, which she soon found unnecessary, as the cattle stayed outdoors year-round. And when she constructed concrete vats to dip her cattle in a chemical bath to kill ticks, the snickers turned to outright laughter. Ticks had long been an insurmountable problem for cattlemen, who believed that they originated from inside the animal and that nothing could be done about them.

Yet it soon became apparent that one rancher—Bertha Palmer—had cattle that were tick-free. In 1923, the Florida legislature passed a law requiring all cattle owners to dip their cattle for ticks, and gradually the pest was eliminated.

UNDERSEA TELEGRAPH CABLE TO CUBA

When the Civil War ended in 1865, the nation, for the first time in four years, turned its attention to other matters. The invention of the telegraph had made instant communication possible with other parts of the country. Now it was time to look to other parts of the world. Few people would have thought that the still largely untamed state of Florida would be one of the leaders in undersea telegraphy.

Cable to England

In 1866, after several failed attempts, Cyrus West Field succeeded in laying the world's first undersea telegraph cable, between the United States and Great Britain. Whereas communication between America and Europe had once taken a month, that time was now shortened to a second or two. The concept of instant communication between countries separated by a vast expanse of water continued to fascinate the public. Even before Fields had accomplished his feat, others had begun to take steps to lay another cable to connect with lands to the south. After dealing with much red tape on the part of both the Spanish government and the Florida legislature, a former Union army general, William F. "Baldy" Smith, was able to plan the construction of the first undersea telegraph cable to Cuba. The International Ocean Telegraph Company (IOTC) would begin at Gainesville, Florida, build the cable across mostly wilderness land to Punta Rassa, near Fort Myers, then go under the ocean to Key West, and from there to Havana, Cuba. To accomplish the task, 75 crewmen grouped into 10 teams, along with their supplies and 350 miles of copper wire, were assembled in New York and sent to Florida.

Just the land-based portion of the project was a mammoth undertaking. The cable had to go over 200 miles of mostly unexplored land inhabited by alligators and rattlesnakes. The IOTC crews often had to wade through swamps of waist-deep water, not knowing what lurked beneath the surface.

Success

The project's supervisors decided to lay the first part of the undersea cable from Key West to Cuba. After a week of preparations, a ship left Key West on August 3, 1867, laying cable as she went, and arrived off the Cuban coast two days later. By August 19, the cable had been successfully spliced, set up, and connected. The entire operation, from the time it was started by Baldy Smith in Gainesville, had taken only a little more than two years.

On August 21, Key West's mayor, E. O. Gwynn, telegraphed Captain-General Joaquin del Manzano in Havana: "As our facilities of intercourse improve, so may our mutual interests and prosperity increase." Manzano's reply: "I celebrate this happy event, which, giving us more rapid communication, will powerfully contribute toward the development of our mutual interests and prosperity."

But although Key West could now communicate with Havana, it was disconnected from the rest of Florida. An outbreak of yellow fever slowed construction, and it was not until May 1871 that the cable was laid from Key West to Punta Rassa.

In 1870, the IOTC expanded its telegraphic network by connecting Cuba with Jamaica and Panama, and later added cables to Puerto Rico and Trinidad. The Florida–Cuba line from Punta Rassa remained in use until 1942. In 1957, the IOTC was absorbed by Western Union.

Commerce and Industry

MAJOR FILM CAPITAL

While motion pictures were first produced in New York, Chicago, and Philadelphia, it was not until producer Samuel Long moved his Kalem Studios to Florida in 1908 that a major film capital was established. The movies' coming of age was not in Hollywood, but in Jacksonville.

As demand grew for more and better movies, Long could see he needed a climate that would allow him to shoot all year long. He

Actors look out to sea in an early movie filmed in Jacksonville. *Courtesy of the Florida State Archives*

chose Jacksonville, sight unseen, because at that time it was the largest city in Florida and a center of finance and manufacturing. It was easy to reach by rail and by ship. As for scenic backdrops, the only thing missing was mountains. Nearby were plenty of rivers, wide beaches, forests, and lush orange groves. Land and labor costs were relatively low, and the city of Jacksonville welcomed new industry. It would be several years before lighting technology would make indoor filming possible, and since Jacksonville averaged 272 days of clear sunshine per year, it was clearly the best choice. A severe winter in the Northeast in 1908 shut down film production for several months and finally erased any doubt.

Instant Success

The first company to arrive and stay for any length of time was Kalem Studios. In 1909, the success of its film *A Florida Feud: Or, Love in the Everglades* brought national acclaim. The studio began cranking out action thrillers and usually had two in production every week. By 1914, the company boasted the world's largest outdoor stage and an indoor studio with a $20,000 lighting system. Such well-known actors as Lionel Barrymore, Oliver Hardy, and George M. Cohan were hired to star.

Other major film companies began to move to Florida. By 1916, Jacksonville was home to about 30 studios, and moviemaking was its leading industry. More than 1,000 actors lived in the city or in surrounding areas. Many film executives relocated with the intention of becoming full-time residents, and some took an active role in civic affairs. It looked like the film industry was in Florida to stay.

Trouble Brewing

It wasn't long, however, before problems began to crop up. When America entered World War I in 1917, supplies of raw film became scarce. Many theaters nationwide closed due to a deadly influenza epidemic, and coal shortages brought on by a spell of freezing weather in the Northeast closed even more. Several studios went bankrupt. Tempers were short, and rival film companies began to have legal problems.

Townspeople, who at first had welcomed the "movie people," were unsympathetic. Many locals had found some of the films offensive because they portrayed southerners as flighty and lazy. They had begun to tire of high-speed chases and of false alarms being set so fire engines could be filmed racing through the city. Other townspeople disapproved of the studio employees' practice of working on the Sabbath. After the war, only three small companies remained. The movie industry was off to Hollywood.

Still in the Movies

Although it no longer had a film capital, Florida continued to play a major role in motion pictures. Until 1926, when the collapse of the land boom ended the practice, Hollywood filmmakers used southern Florida's beaches in movies about the South Seas and desert sands. In the 1980s, decades after the industry moved to California, Florida once again began to attract

---

MONEY MAKERS

When studios film on location in Florida, it's a tremendous source of revenue. About 40 percent of a movie's budget is spent in the community where the filming takes place. When *Jaws 2* was filmed in Navarre, the cast and crew spent $750,000 on hotel rooms, $200,000 at a lumber yard, $170,000 for local people to serve as extras, $250,000 for cars, $200,000 for boats, and $18,000 in a local hardware store for paint.

major studios such as Universal, Disney, and MGM. By 1995, it had become the third-largest filmmaking state in the nation.

Some popular movies made in Florida were: *Thirty Seconds Over Tokyo*, 1944; *The Yearling*, 1946; *Twelve O'Clock High*, 1949; *The Rose Tattoo*, 1955; *A Hole in the Head*, 1959; *The Day of the Dolphin*, 1973; *The Godfather, Part II*, 1974; *Jaws 2*, 1978; *The Champ*, 1979; *Body Heat*, 1981; *Ghost Story*, 1981; *Scarface*, 1983; *Cocoon*, 1985; *Days of Thunder*, 1990; *Edward Scissorhands*, 1990; *The Lion King*, 1994; *Apollo 13*, 1995; *The Birdcage*, 1996; *The Truman Show*, 1998.

SPONGE INDUSTRY

When a Key West freighter took a load of sponges to New York in 1849, they were purchased almost immediately. The captain returned to Florida and told local sponge fishermen he would buy all the sponges they could bring him, as long as they were of high quality. That was the

Sponge Industry, Key West, Florida

Buyers inspect the sponge crop in Key West. *Courtesy of the Florida State Archives* beginning of the sponge industry in the United States. It thrived in Key West for 50 years.

But by the end of the 19th century, the sponge beds were drying up, due in part to the attacks of a microscopic fungus. Some people also blamed the construction of Henry Flagler's overseas railroad for somehow disturbing the natural environment. Others said sponge fishermen were coming down from Tarpon Springs and ruthlessly trampling the beds while scooping up the sponges in heavy nets.

Move to Tarpon Springs

The industry moved to Tarpon Springs in the 1890s after John K. Cheney, a Philadelphia businessman, came to promote the area as an exclusive winter resort. Cheney discovered that the Gulf of Mexico, north of Tampa Bay, was one of the few places in the world where the species of natural sponges suitable for commercial use were found. He felt that harvesting sponges could be a lucrative enterprise and launched several sponge-fishing boats, which retrieved sponges with long-handled hooks, into the gulf. The practice, called "hooking," could be done only in very clear water that was less than 45 feet deep.

While on a business trip to New York around 1905, Cheney met John Cocoris, a native of Greece whose family had been in the sponge business for generations. Cheney persuaded Cocoris to quit his job as a buyer for a Greek sponge company and move to Tarpon Springs to work for him. Cocoris showed Cheney a secondhand diving suit he had brought from New York, complete with an air hose and a steel-and-glass helmet. He explained the practice of diving for sponges in deep water, where the beds were more plentiful and the sponges of higher quality, as this was the method most commonly used in his homeland. He persuaded his employer to bring more Greek sponge divers into the area, and by the end of 1906, about 1,500 of them were living and working in Tarpon Springs. By 1908, sponging was a million-dollar enterprise.

DIVING FOR THE CROSS

Each year on January 6, thousands of visitors come to Tarpon Springs to see a colorful ceremony that climaxes in young men diving for a cross thrown into the Gulf of Mexico. This is the celebration of the festival of Epiphany, said to be the commemoration of the baptism of Christ. It is the world's largest celebration of this feast day.

Growth and Prosperity

The sponge industry grew and prospered, reaching its peak in the 1930s. In 1939, a disease hit the beds, reducing the crop of sponges for decades. In the 1980s, divers once again found healthy sponge beds, and the industry was revived. Today, the beds are the healthiest and most plentiful in years. Tarpon Springs has regained its reputation as the largest natural-sponge market in the world, with annual revenues of more than $5 million.

CIGAR INDUSTRY

Like the sponge industry, the cigar industry in America began in Key West and flourished there during the 1800s. Also like the sponge industry, it declined around the turn of the 20th century and moved to another Florida city.

In 1831, William H. Wall opened the country's first cigar factory on Front Street in Key West. But it would be over three decades before the Cuban Revolution of 1868 brought to the city large numbers of Cuban exiles who built many more factories and made Key West the cigar-manufacturing capital of the United States.

> ### *RISE AND FALL*
>
> After losing its two major industries, sponges and cigars, then enduring the Great Depression and the massive 1935 hurricane, Key West, which at one time had been the wealthiest city per capita in the United States, became the poorest.

Cuban Influx

By 1870, dozens of Cubans fleeing the violence and bloodshed in their country were arriving weekly in Key West, and by 1873 they composed the majority of the city's population. Even though their 10-year war against Spain resulted in failure, the exiles, thousands of whom were skilled cigar makers, continued to come to Florida for the remainder of the century.

When Don Vicente Martinez Ybor, a Spanish-born Cuban cigar magnate, fled to Key West in 1869, he took advantage of this huge, ready-made labor pool to build up the city's small cigar industry. Within 10 years, Key West became known as the home of the "clear Havana cigar industry of the United States," and the city continued to attract more cigar workers.

In 1886, a disastrous fire swept Key West and destroyed many of the factories. By that time, Cuban immigrants and native Key Westers had begun to find themselves in fierce competition for jobs. The transplanted Cuban workers, accustomed to the militant trade unions in their native country, banded together to secure better wages and working conditions. The fire and the hostile labor relations led the industry into a decline. Ybor and New York cigar manufacturer Ignacio Haya decided to relocate.

Move to Tampa

After looking at several cities on the Gulf of Mexico, Ybor and Haya chose Tampa. Railroad and steamship lines had recently been brought to the city by industrialist Henry Plant, and its humid climate was conducive to tobacco rolling. Ybor obtained a 40-acre parcel of land northeast of downtown Tampa, where he relocated his thriving Key West cigar business. Soon Spanish cigar manufacturers and German box makers flocked to the area, now known as Ybor City. Tampa enticed 40 major cigar companies from other cities to do the same.

REMNANTS

Remnants of the cigar industry exist today in Key West. At the Caribbean Cigar Factory, Cuban workers still hand-roll cigars, just as their forebears did a century ago.

READERS

In the early days of the cigar industry, all cigars were hand-rolled of the finest Cuban tobacco by skilled workers who had learned their trade in childhood. It was tedious work, and to break the monotony, hired *lectores,* or readers, read magazines and newspapers, even philosophical works and classic novels, to the workers. Many workers said they received the equivalent of a college education from the *lectores.*

El lector (right) reads to workers in an early Tampa cigar factory. *Courtesy of the Florida State Archives*

Tampa became known as the world's leading producer of cigars, and the industry thrived until Fidel Castro came to power in 1959 and Cuba's relationship with the United States became strained. On February 3, 1962, President John F. Kennedy banned all trade between the United States and Cuba. This was disastrous for the Tampa cigar industry, which was dependent on Cuban tobacco. Many factories closed. Today they have been converted into shops, boutiques, business offices, even living quarters and artists' studios. Ybor City retains its colorful Latin charm, and is home to the world-famous Columbia Restaurant, the oldest Cuban restaurant in the United States.

The cigar industry eventually rebounded, and new, modern factories replaced the old ones. Machine-rolling has made for cheaper, mass-produced cigars, but nothing has equaled the quality of the hand-rolled variety. Tampa is no longer a one-industry city, but it is still the leading producer of cigars in the United States.

☀ To Visit: Ybor City State Museum

The Ybor City State Museum and the nearby Cigar Workers' Homes provide a good source of information about the history of the area. The museum is housed in the renovated Ferlita Bakery, which once provided bread for the residents. The Cigar Workers' Homes are frame cottages, once common in the community. Two of the cottages show exhibits of the early cigar industry.

Ybor City State Museum
1818 East 9th Avenue
Ybor City, FL 33605
813-247-6323
Hours: Tuesday-Saturday, 9 A.M.-12 P.M. and 1-5 P.M.
Closed Thanksgiving and Christmas.
Admission charged.

CITRUS-PROCESSING PLANT

When the Florida Fruit Products Company was formed by C. E. Street in 1915, it began operations in the old *Haines City Herald* building on Railroad Avenue. It packed "Street's Pure Grapefruit Juice" in quart-sized glass bottles and shipped them to market in wooden cases.

This Haines City citrus-processing plant used steam for power.
Courtesy of the Florida State Archives

But it soon became clear that a building constructed to house a newspaper plant would not do for citrus processing. In 1916, Florida Fruit Products built the first citrus-processing plant in America in Haines City.

The four-story, brick plant operated entirely by steam, with electricity used only for lighting. When the grapefruit came in, they traveled on belts pulled by pulleys to the top floor. Workers cut them in half and juiced them by hand on crude reamers. The juice then flowed down to the lower floors for processing. The Florida Fruit Products building later housed two other citrus-processing companies.

PHOSPHATE MINING

After tourism and citrus, mining for phosphate is Florida's third-largest industry. It began in the 1880s after Captain J. Francis LeBaron, an engineer with the U.S. Army Corps of Engineers, discovered phosphate pebbles in the Peace River, south of Fort Meade. It was the first discovery in the United States of the valuable mineral.

Although LeBaron had been sent to the area to determine the feasibility of opening a navigable waterway for steamboats, his discovery of bone phosphate (or, as it would later be called, river pebble phosphate) had far more significance.

Partnership

Phosphate, formed from marine organisms at a prehistoric time when Florida was covered by the ocean, is most highly valued for its use in the production of fertilizer. LeBaron tried to interest potential investors in his find, but he met with no success until word reached T. S. Morehead, one of his associate engineers with the army. In May 1887, Morehead purchased a tract of 200 acres near Arcadia, but left the area when an epidemic of yellow fever threatened to move upstate from Key West.

Workers haul phosphate in an early mine in central Florida. *Courtesy of the Florida State Archives*

Later that year, George W. Scott, president of a large fertilizer company in Atlanta, led an expedition to explore the region. His team soon located large deposits of phosphate but, like Morehead, was forced to evacuate by the threat of yellow fever. Scott returned on November 1, 1889, and began mining with a reorganized company he had named the Peace River Phosphate Company. In the meantime, Morehead had purchased an additional 400 acres and started his own company, the Arcadia Phosphate Company. The two men agreed that Scott would purchase Morehead's entire output of phosphate and Morehead would dry it and ship it to Atlanta.

Boom and Bust

"Phosphate fever" soon spread through the entire Peace River Valley, and 18 plants were set up from Bartow to Hickory Bluff. By 1892, production had reached 354,000 tons, up from 2,813 tons in 1889. Land prices soared, and speculators and wildcatters descended on the area. By 1895, 400 phosphate companies were operating in Florida.

Just five years later, only 50 of those companies remained. The others had become victims of a nationwide recession, new competition, soaring costs, and the great freezes of 1894 and 1895, which had reduced the demand for fertilizer. By 1900, the phosphate boom had ended.

A century later, however, phosphate is once again big business. It has been a mixed blessing: a huge source of income, but also an ecological disaster. The mines have left ugly scars in the land and played havoc with the environment, destroying wildlife and drying up waterways. Fortunately, the newer, more ecologically aware companies have committed to making the preservation of the environment a priority.

RYDER TRUCK

When high school student Jim Ryder landed a summer job at a Miami Beach construction site, hauling cement and concrete blocks in a wheelbarrow for 25 cents an hour, he felt lucky to get it. It was 1932, and jobs were scarce. Then a fellow student told Ryder he was making 10 cents more per hour delivering the same materials in a truck, sparking an idea that led to the formation of one of the world's leading transportation-services companies.

In 1933, Ryder managed to save $35 to buy his first truck, a black 1931 Model A Ford. At a time when store clerks were putting in a 60-hour week to earn $6 and banks were failing all over the country, jobs for the fledgling entrepreneur came hard. But Ryder viewed the obstacles as challenges. Since the depressed economy made it difficult for many business owners to purchase their own trucks, he saw a need he could fill. He put himself and his truck up for hire, and he found that there was enough of a demand for his services that in 1934 he was able to double the size of his fleet with a second truck, a 1934 Ford V-8. His business continued to grow, and by 1937 Ryder had 15 trucks in service.

Truck Leasing

Ryder entered the truck-leasing business in 1937, when Champagne Velvet Beer agreed to lease five trucks. The business skyrocketed as he landed accounts with such giants as Anheuser-Busch and the *Miami Herald*, which today is the company's oldest account. By 1949, Ryder Truck Lines had five branches and 450 trucks. In 1957, the company's truck-leasing and rental operations expanded into Canada.

The 1970s were a decade of tremendous growth for the firm as it acquired other companies, such as M&G Convoy, Complete Auto Transit, Southern Underwriters, and Truckstops of America, and expanded into Europe. Today it has operations in Mexico and South America and is recognized as one of the world's top 100 diversified companies.

OFFICE DEPOT

In 1985, the office-products industry was dominated by small, independent stores that marked up prices by as much as 50 percent. In that year, though, a small group of experienced retailers decided to apply warehouse retailing, which had been used successfully by the home-improvement store chain Home Depot for several years, to office products. In 1986, the first Office Depot opened in Fort Lauderdale. The company, which started with one store in Florida, would ultimately open stores throughout the nation and around the world.

Success

The new Office Depot was an immediate success. The next year, 10 new stores were added and, under the direction of David I. Fuentes as chairman and chief executive officer, the company went public. By December 1990, it had a total of 122 stores. In 1991, a merger with California-based Office Club, another office-products superstore chain, brought in 51 additional stores and solidified Office Depot's position as the largest office-products retailer in North America.

By 1992, the chain had expanded into Canada by acquiring the Great Canadian Office Supplies Warehouse chain, converting its five stores to Office Depots, and adding more around the country. It soon moved into Europe and Japan. Today there are nearly 1,000 Office Depots throughout the world.

MODERN SUPERMARKET

After 1940, when George W. Jenkins closed his two existing Publix stores in Winter Haven and opened a new one, grocery shopping would never be the same. The new store was touted as a state-of-the-art "food palace," with art deco architecture, electric-eye doors, air conditioning, piped-in music, fluorescent lighting, and aisles eight feet wide. The new Winter Haven Publix would be a place "where shopping is a pleasure," and that became its slogan. It was the first modern supermarket in the world.

Publix opened in 1940 as the world's first modern super-market. *Courtesy of Publix Super Markets, Inc.*

Jenkins, son of the owner of a small country grocery store in Georgia, had come to St. Petersburg at the age of 17 with nine dollars in his pocket. His goal was to become an electrical engineer, but to support himself in the meantime, he took a job as a clerk in a Piggly Wiggly grocery store. Two months later, he was made manager. He saw to it that the store was always immaculate and a pleasant place to shop. Under his management, prices were competitive and the shelves were well stocked. Sales quadrupled, and Jenkins was promoted to manager of a larger store in Winter Haven.

On His Own

In 1930, he opened his own store and named it Publix, after a chain of movie theaters. It was so successful that in 1933, the Piggly Wiggly store next door was forced out of business. Jenkins opened a second store on the other side of town in 1935, and a third shortly thereafter in Lake Wales.

When the new Publix supermarket, constructed of stucco, marble, and tile, opened in 1940, shoppers came from miles around just to see the electric-eye doors. Publix had begun a trend: owners of other food-store chains quickly realized that they would have to modernize their stores in order to compete. In 1944, Jenkins purchased the 19 stores in the All-American food-store chain, which was based in Lakeland, and moved his headquarters to Lakeland. Today the Publix complex covers 2 million square feet and includes bakery and dairy-processing plants, a 108,000-square-foot frozen-food warehouse, a data-processing center, and administrative offices. Five other major distribution centers now operate throughout Florida.

George Jenkins died in 1996. His son, Howard Jenkins, now chairman of the board and chief executive officer of the Publix chain, has maintained the success of Publix by carrying on his father's vision and adding tech-nological advances. Publix was the first food-store chain to use electronic scanning devices in all of its stores. Today it is a *Fortune* 500 company, with 664 stores in Florida and neighboring states.

Firsts for Nature Lovers

NATIONAL WILDLIFE REFUGE

For almost a century, Pelican Island, in the Indian River Lagoon off Sebastian, has been a refuge for the once endangered brown pelican, as well as for herons, egrets, and spoonbills. It was the first of almost 500 refuges and parks, totaling more than 90 million acres, that today make up the National Wildlife Refuge System, the world's largest network of lands managed for wildlife.

In the latter half of the 19th century, the birds' colorful feathers were much sought after in the fashion industry. By the end of the century, the bird population on the five-acre island had been decimated by plume hunters, so in 1901 the State of Florida outlawed the killing of nongame birds. The American Ornithologists' Union hired Paul Krogel, a German immigrant and boat builder, as a warden to enforce the new law. Krogel, a strong proponent of saving the birds, took the job for a salary of one dollar a month. He made sure visitors could not shoot the pelicans or take their eggs, but there was no way to prevent them from coming to the island and disturbing the birds.

The Beginnings

Ornithologist Frank Chapman, an associate curator at the American Museum of Natural History, was a frequent visitor to

Wood storks tend
to their young on
Pelican Island.
*Courtesy of
Delinda Karheim,*
Florida Today

the east coast of Florida in the 1890s. In 1898, he began the most thorough study ever made of the brown pelican and visited Pelican Island often. His published works about the distress of the birds in the Indian River Lagoon helped him gain the support of several influential people, and even persuaded his good friend President Teddy Roosevelt of the importance of preserving the small plot of land. On March 14, 1903, Roosevelt proclaimed Pelican Island a National Wildlife Refuge and barred all visitors.

Preservation of the Island

In 1968, when the Fish and Wildlife Service entered into an agreement with the State of Florida to manage the submerged land around the island, the Pelican Island Refuge consisted of only 10 acres, which included several acres of underwater bottomlands. While it now encompasses 4,640 acres of bottomlands and mangrove islands and a 395-acre buffer on an adjacent barrier island, the island itself has dwindled from 5 acres to $2\frac{1}{2}$. When U.S. Secretary of the Interior Bruce Babbit toured the refuge in 1999, he remarked, "In 1903 the threat was poaching. Now it's encroachment by development. We need to fulfill our obligation and make sure there is enough space for the birds and the people." He said Congress needs to commit to saving the island and protecting the wildlife for future generations.

Today, Pelican Island is home to the brown pelican and the endangered wood stork. Twelve other species of birds nest there, including egrets, herons, and cormorants, and about 45 other species come from nearby islands to forage or roost. The green sea turtle, the loggerhead sea turtle, and the manatee, all threatened or endangered species, can also be found at the refuge. It was named a National Historic Landmark in 1963 and a Wetland of International Importance in 1993.

New Projects

Projects are under way today to help preserve the island. Mangroves are being planted to fight erosion, and invasive plants are being removed. The U.S. Fish and Wildlife Service hopes to buy land for a buffer to prevent nearby commercial development and is also working on a 15-year management plan for the property.

Several facilities are now being planned for Melbourne Beach, a half-mile from Pelican Island, so visitors may observe and photograph the wildlife. They include a viewing tower, an information station, and walking trails.

 To Visit: Pelican Island

Pelican Island is in the Indian River Lagoon between Sebastian, on U.S. Route 1 on the mainland, and Melbourne Beach, on a barrier island east of the lagoon. Boat tours leave from both places. Each year from early October through June 1, the *Inlet Explorer* offers a two-hour tour with a park ranger as guide.

The Inlet Explorer
9502 Highway A1A South
Melbourne Beach, FL 32951
321-952-1126
Admission charged.

UNDERSEA PARK

At 56,000 acres, John Pennekamp Coral Reef State Park is Florida's largest. As most national and state parks are, it is a place of breathtaking wonder and scenic grandeur. But don't count on seeing it from a car window. The best way is with scuba gear or snorkel and fins. With all but 2,350 of its acres under water, Pennekamp is the nation's first undersea state park.

The park was created in 1960, partly to preserve Florida's living coral reef, the only one in the continental United States. Formed from the limestone skeletons of billions of tiny, soft-bodied sea creatures, the reef stretches 125 miles through the Atlantic Ocean from just north of Elliot Key to

A snorkeler inspects *Christ of the Deep* at John Pennekamp Coral Reef State Park. *Courtesy of the Key Largo Chamber of Commerce*

Key West. It is home to living coral animals that flourish in a fantasyland of brilliant colors. Divers who explore one of the several different sections of the reef at the park can also see barracuda, moray eels, parrotfish, grouper, snapper, lobster, rays, and loggerhead and green sea turtles. Several different kinds of coral, including the delicate staghorn coral and large star and brain coral formations, add to the spectacle.

By the 1950s, this undersea treasure was being threatened with destruction by divers and sightseers. While many were content to photograph or simply gaze in awe at its splendor, others wanted to chip off pieces of the reef to display in their living rooms. Still others speared the fish to take back to their boats. Even worse, curio vendors would dynamite large chunks of the reef, bleach it white, and sell it along the roadside.

Preservation of the Reef

Fortunately, those with foresight and an appreciation for the ecological importance of the reef prevailed. In 1960, the park, which contains a 21-mile segment of the reef, was opened in Key Largo and named for John D. Pennekamp, an associate editor of the *Miami Herald,* who for more than 20 years used the power of his pen to fight for conservation of Florida's underwater natural resources. In John Pennekamp Coral Reef State Park, there would be no spearfishing or coral collecting, and preservation of the reef would be a top priority.

The park is a favorite with scuba divers and snorkelers, many of whom spend several days seeing sights that can be found nowhere else in the world. In the 18th and 19th centuries, the area around the reef became a graveyard for many large ships sunk by pirates and hurricanes. Divers can visit several wrecked ships, such as *The City of Washington,* which was launched in 1877 to carry passengers between New York and Havana. Snorkelers can choose from five sites. One of the most popular is Grecian Rocks, where the water is so shallow that the reef sometimes breaks the surface. Another site is Dry Rocks, where *Christ of the Deep,* a nine-foot-tall, 4,000-pound underwater statue of Christ, stands just outside the park in the

The only living coral reef in the United States attracts both divers and snorkelers at John Pennekamp Coral Reef State Park. *Courtesy of the Key Largo Chamber of Commerce*

Key Largo Marine Sanctuary. Positioned with arms upright, it is a replica of a statue 50 feet under the Mediterranean Sea near Genoa, Italy, which was built in 1954 as a shrine for sailors and those who had lost loved ones at sea.

Visitors who prefer to stay dry can take a tour in a glass-bottomed boat or rent a canoe, a motorboat, or a sailboat. The land portion of the park offers hiking trails and picnic and camping grounds. A 30,000-gallon aquarium in the visitors center holds a living reef and endemic fish and plant life, showing a sample of what snorkelers see under the water.

To Visit: John Pennekamp Coral Reef State Park

John Pennekamp Coral Reef State Park
Mile Marker 102.5
Overseas Highway
Key Largo, FL 33037
305-451-1202
Hours: Daily, 9 A.M.-3 P.M.
Admission free, but there are charges for boat tours, self-guided tours, and equipment rental.

NATIONAL PARK CHOSEN FOR ITS BIOLOGY

In a vast plane of sawgrass and water, a landscape as flat as any on earth, the Florida Everglades teems with life—on land, under water, and in the sky. Many of its life forms can be found nowhere else in the United States. It is for this reason that in 1947 President Harry Truman dedicated the southern tip of Florida as Everglades National Park, the first national park to be protected for its plant and animal life rather than for its scenic grandeur.

The idea of designating a large tract of land in the Everglades as a national park was proposed as far back as the 1920s. One of the strongest proponents was Ernest F. Coe, a Coconut Grove landscape artist whom conservationist Marjory Stoneman Douglas described as "on fire with the passion of an idea that would possess him for the rest of his life." Douglas, who later wrote *The Everglades: River of Grass*, was the daughter of the editor of the *Miami Herald*, Frank B. Stoneman. Coe enlisted Stoneman and other influential people, such as horticulturist David Fairchild, to help him with his cause. In 1930, a seven-member team that included Horace Albright, director of the National Park Service, toured the lower Everglades, then delivered a report to the U.S. secretary of the interior that the team was strongly in favor of establishing a park to protect the nation's only subtropical wilderness. The State of Florida conveyed 850,000 acres of state property to the National Park Service and appropriated $2 million for the purchase of additional land for the park.

Destruction

The main reason for the designation of a portion of the Everglades as a national park was to halt or at least slow down the destruction that had been going on for decades. Agricultural and urban development has altered about 30 percent of the Everglades, and another 50 percent has been changed to create water-conservation areas. Many plants and animals have been driven out as their habitat has been destroyed.

Despite the destruction, the Everglades remains a place of rich biological treasures. Islands with thick vegetation and clusters of trees called hammocks dot the landscape. The fresh water flowing into salty Florida Bay makes for a variety of watery habitats for many different species of plant and animal life. Here palm trees grow 100 feet tall. A myriad of orchids, air plants, and ferns—many seen nowhere else in the United States—decorate tree branches. Sea turtles still lay their eggs on the sandy Cape Sable beach, and black bears and panthers stalk their prey through centuries-old cypress trees. Alligators bask in the sun and bellow their mating calls in the spring. The rare American crocodile also makes its home here; the Everglades is the only place in the world where alligators and crocodiles live together. The rich bird life includes ospreys, brown pelicans, bald eagles, roseate spoonbills, snowy egrets, sandhill cranes, and wild turkeys. This abundance of wildlife prompted the United States Travel Service in 1974 to name the Florida Everglades, along with the Grand Canyon and Niagara Falls, one of the seven natural wonders of the United States of America.

 ### To Visit: Everglades National Park

Everglades National Park can be toured by automobile, bicycle, boat, or canoe. The park has camping facilities, a motel, and a marina, with boat tours and boat and canoe rentals. Visitors should bring sunscreen and insect repellent.

Everglades National Park
40001 State Road 9336
Homestead, FL 33034
305-242-7700
Park entrance fees charged.

THE GLADES WILL BE PRESERVED

On December 11, 2000, President Bill Clinton signed the $7.8 billion, 25-year Everglades restoration project into law. This will restore the natural flow of water in the Everglades and gradually reverse the effects of decades of destruction.

LAND BRIDGE

Motorists on Interstate 75 near Ocala often do a double take when they see a bridge over the busy highway with trees growing out of the top. Built at a cost of $3.4 million and dedicated in opening ceremonies on September 30, 2000, the beautiful Cross Florida Greenway Land Bridge is one of Florida's newest firsts, the first man-made land bridge in the United States.

The bridge now makes it possible for hikers, bicyclists, and horseback riders to travel from the Gulf of Mexico to the St. Johns River, as much as 110 miles, through scenic woodlands containing rivers, lakes, and wetlands, without having to stop for a passing car. Blending natural and man-made features, the bridge links the east and west sides of the Marjorie Harris Carr Cross Florida Greenway, which was divided by highway construction in the 1960s. It is the first land bridge in the world built with people, not animals, in mind; still, it has turned out to be a boon for the deer, foxes, possums, and raccoons whose tracks reveal they have been safely scampering across it after dark.

The trail was built to blend in with the natural environment on both sides of the 17-foot-high, 520-foot-wide bridge. Trees and shrubbery are not planted symmetrically or in a pattern, but grow just as they do in the

Construction begins on the Cross Florida Greenway Land Bridge. *Courtesy of the Florida Department of Transportation*

wild. Recycled materials, such as crushed clamshells and pine-needle mulch, form a path through what appears to be wilderness land. White fieldstone walls on either side of the path hold back hundreds of tons of topsoil planted with native oaks, saw palmettos, and pine.

Boondoggle

Ironically, the site for the bridge was once the setting for one of the world's greatest boondoggles, the ill-fated Cross Florida Barge Canal, a proposed water link between the Atlantic Ocean and the Gulf of Mexico.

Visitors cross the Cross Florida Greenway Land Bridge on its opening day, September 30, 2000. *Courtesy of Cindy Skop, Ocala Star-Banner*

The project, controversial since its inception, was vehemently opposed by those who foresaw permanent damage to the fragile environment, especially to the scenic Ocklawaha River, the crystalline Silver Springs, and the underground aquifer that provides Florida's drinking water. Nonetheless, in 1935, President Franklin D. Roosevelt authorized $5 million to begin construction. Work was halted in the 1940s, as money was needed for the war effort, and began again in 1960 with federal authorization. Environmentalists won a victory in 1971 when, with the waterway one-third completed and almost $50 million already spent, President Richard M. Nixon ordered all work suspended. But proponents of the canal questioned this order, declaring it illegal, and it was not until November 28, 1990, that the project was officially deauthorized and nature lovers could proclaim: "At long last the wicked ditch is dead."

Alan Bryant, chief engineer for the land bridge project, is justifiably proud of what he and his team have created. "It was awesome to be a part of it," he said. "We took something that would have destroyed the environment and turned it into a beautiful bridge that people will enjoy for generations."

The new bridge has started a trend. A second land bridge is already under construction near Palm Coast, and officials from other states who have visited the site are considering the idea.

FEDERAL PRISON ON AN ISLAND

The Dry Tortugas, so named by Ponce de León for their lack of drinking water and for the large numbers of turtles (*tortugas*) he found there, lie 68 miles due west of Key West. On Garden Key in the Tortugas rises a gigantic fortress named Fort Jefferson. During the Civil War it became a federal prison, the first in the United States to be built on an island.

In 1846, construction began on the mammoth, six-sided masonry structure. The huge center courtyard was surrounded by walls 45 feet high and 8 feet thick. The fort was built almost to the edges of the island and today still looks as if it rises full-blown from the sea. It was to be part of a string of coastal fortifications along the Atlantic and Gulf coasts that were to ward off enemy attacks by sea. It occupied a strategic position between the Atlantic Ocean, the Gulf of Mexico, and the Caribbean Sea. Although it was never completed, Fort Jefferson is America's largest 19th-century coastal fort.

Civil War Prison

By the time the Civil War broke out in 1861, Fort Jefferson was already obsolete as a fortress due to developments in the weaponry of the time. Construction was halted, and the huge structure became a federal prison for deserters and other criminals. Its best-known inmate was Dr. Samuel Mudd, who set the broken leg of John Wilkes Booth, the assassin of Abraham Lincoln. Mudd claimed he had no knowledge of the crime and was simply carrying out his duties as a physician. Still, in 1865, he was banished to the isolated fort, where he was imprisoned with three other men who were considered conspirators in the assassination. Conditions were abominable, and one of the men described the prison bread as "a mixture of flour, bugs, sticks, and dirt," and the meat as "so rotten that dogs ran from it." When a yellow fever epidemic struck the prison, killing many of the inmates and the garrison surgeon, Dr. Mudd was summoned to help stop the rising death toll.

After working day and night for weeks, he was finally able to bring the disease under control. Prison officials praised his work and petitioned authorities for his release. In 1869, he was pardoned by President Andrew Johnson and returned to his Maryland home, only to find "his name was Mudd" among former friends and supporters. He died in 1885, at the age of 49.

Today, Garden Key is a paradise for bird lovers, snorkelers, and campers, a place to experience what Florida was like before builders and developers took over. The Tortugas' large flocks of birds, which include gulls, cormorants, pelicans, terns, and peregrine falcons, inspired John James Audubon, a famous painter of birds, to sail out to the island in 1832 to study them. Snorkelers will find 442 species of fish swimming in crystal-clear water against an eye-catching backdrop of brain coral, sea fans, and turtle grass.

UNDERSEA HOTEL

When a well-heeled, young businessman recently decided to give his bride the wedding and honeymoon of a lifetime, he called Jules' Undersea Lodge in Key Largo. For $1,000 a night the lucky couple could say their vows while watching an angelfish swim by their porthole. They and their guests would then be treated to champagne and the world's only underwater wedding cake. Afterward, they would start their life together with exclusive use of the two-bedroom hotel, where they would be treated to scrumptious meals, fresh flowers, mood music, and caviar.

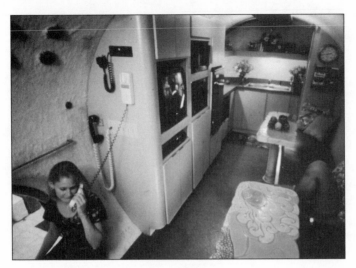

A couple relaxes on their honey-moon at Jules' Undersea Lodge. *Courtesy of Murry Sill*

There was, however, one requirement. Both bride and groom, as well as all of the wedding guests and the minister who would perform the ceremony, would have to be certified aquanauts, as the only way to enter the hotel is by scuba diving. The world's first underwater hotel is five fathoms (30 feet) under the surface of the sea.

The Beginnings

While the hotel might sound like a fun spot for tourists, it has a much more serious side. Located in a natural mangrove lagoon that it shares with MarineLab, an underwater research and education laboratory, it began life in the early 1970s as La Chalupa Research Lab and was used to explore the continental shelf off the coast of Puerto Rico. With state-of-the-art equipment, La Chalupa was the most innovative research laboratory of its time. In 1986, two former research assistants, Ian Koblick and Neil Monney,

RESEARCH

From time to time, research projects are still conducted at Jules' Undersea Lodge. Because of the similarities between outer space and the inner space of the sea, NASA has used it for exploring preliminary preparations for extended space travel.

transformed the laboratory into a luxury hotel and named it for Jules Verne, author of *Twenty Thousand Leagues Under the Sea.*

The Emerald Lagoon is not only home to Jules' but is a natural nursery area for many reef fish. Parrotfish, barracuda, and snapper often peer in the portholes, and anemones, sponges, and oysters are everywhere. Guests of the lodge can leisurely explore their underwater habitat with 100-foot "hookah" lines instead of heavy scuba tanks. The lines are a remnant of La Chalupa's deep ocean exploration, which required much more air than a scuba tank could supply.

Jules' is the first place in the world where the average citizen can experience what living under the sea is like, something that was once only a dream of science fiction writers. While it still functions as a research lab, the hotel has all the comforts of its landlocked counterparts: telephone, air conditioning, hot showers, stereo music, TV with VCR, and a fully stocked galley.

Rates begin at $225 per person per day, including meals. Guests who opt for the $325-per-day "Luxury Aquanaut Package" receive training to earn an aquanaut certificate, and also enjoy gourmet meals. They are served by a staff that remains on duty 24 hours a day and includes a "mer-chef" who scubas to the hotel to prepare and serve dinner. All guests have unlimited diving privileges.

More to Come

While Jules' is the first and at the present time the only underwater hotel, it won't be the last. The owners won't give specifics, but they say they have been approached by developers from all over the world who plan to build larger, more comfortable hotels, some with portholes six feet in diameter so guests can enjoy the spectacular views.

As Dr. Monney puts it, "Here is a new step for mankind, the advent of undersea living, the taming of the last frontier on Earth . . . inner space."

☼ To Visit: Jules' Undersea Lodge

Jules' Undersea Lodge
51 Shoreland Drive (Mile Marker 103.2)
Key Largo, FL 33037
305-453-0000

Festivals and Places to Go

OCEANARIUM

Other oceanariums may be bigger and grander, but Marineland of Florida, near St. Augustine, is definitely worth a visit. In 1938, the attraction, then known as Marine Studios, opened as the world's first underwater motion picture studio. The word *oceanarium* was coined to describe this place where different forms of marine life lived together as they do in the sea.

The new theme park was designed to allow marine life to be photographed and studied easily. Built within a few feet of the ocean, it featured a new water exchange method that drew in seawater after filtering it through beach sand. The result was a man-made environment that came as close as possible to the natural habitat of the fish and other sea life that lived in its huge, three-story-high tank.

The Beginnings

The park had been the brainchild of three men—W. Douglas Burden, great-great-grandson of railroad magnate Cornelius Vanderbilt; his cousin, movie producer Cornelius Vanderbilt Whitney; and Ilia Tolstoy, grandson of Count Leo Tolstoy. Their first plan was to build the park in the sea, enclosing it in a steel net. They later decided to build it on land, with large steel tanks

Dolphins perform at Marineland's jumping-dolphin show. *Courtesy of Marineland of Florida*

containing fresh seawater. Since this was a real first, there were a couple of prickly questions: How would they transport large animals like sharks and dolphins from the ocean to the tanks? Would the animals live peaceably together in the tanks, or would they turn on each other? The founders solved the first problem by building special trucks that could carry large tanks filled with salt water. For the second question, they could only wait and see. Fortunately, there was no problem. The marine animals got along just fine.

Marine Studios was to have three major purposes: it would be a research center, a studio where films featuring sea life could be made, and a tourist attraction. Its first small research facility and the neighboring Whitney Laboratory were used to advance understanding of marine life and for biomedical research. Many nature and feature films were made here, including the 1954 science fiction thriller *Creature from the Black Lagoon.*

Later, when Marine Studios began to be used more as a tourist attraction than as a movie studio, its name was changed to Marineland. The techniques of training dolphins for shows were developed here, and the first dolphin born in captivity made its appearance in 1947. During the 1960s, thousands of people visited each week, making Marineland Florida's most visited attraction.

A Sad Birthday

But when Marineland celebrated its 60th birthday in June 1998, it was not a happy one. Attendance was down, due to several factors, one of which was devastating wildfires that had come perilously close to its tanks. Tourists were traveling on Interstate 95, which kept them 15 miles away from Highway A1A and the beach, where Marineland is located. And Orlando's SeaWorld, with its much more modern facilities and spectacular animal exhibits, was only 85 miles away. It was beginning to look as if Marineland could no longer compete in the industry it had pioneered. Later in 1998, it closed.

But many fans of Marineland believed it was worth saving, and the attraction reopened in March 1999. There is still a lot to see here, and every effort is being made to keep the park open. Cute penguins once again strut their stuff for delighted children, and a sea lion does a balancing act with a ball on its nose. Nineteen dolphins still live at Marineland and perform their graceful flips and leaps in the air. Groups from nearby schools find the park has much to teach them, and Marineland counts on school field

Tourists at Marineland enjoy a dolphin encounter. *Courtesy of Marineland of Florida*

trips to provide a large part of its revenue. The newest feature is the dolphin encounter, in which visitors can actually go into the water with the dolphins for a 1½-hour program run by a trainer.

Rebirth

Recently, things have begun to look up. Perhaps most encouraging is the fact that Jim Jacoby, an Atlanta developer, has purchased 40 acres next to Marineland where he plans to build an upscale hotel and a dolphin-research facility containing a demonstration model of an eco-village of the future. There will be bike paths, foot paths, a spa, and a research and education center. One of the most outstanding features will be a 3-million-gallon pond where autistic children can interact with dolphins. The new complex won't be affiliated with Marineland, but Jacoby plans for the two to be compatible, and it is expected to attract people who will also visit the neighboring attraction.

While Marineland can't compete with SeaWorld and doesn't try, its pace is leisurely and uncrowded, and children can get up-close-and-personal with the animals. Admission prices are a fraction of those at Orlando's gigantic attraction. A visitor recently remarked, "I first came here in 1947 with my parents, and we loved it. Now I want my grandson to see it."

☀ To Visit: Marineland of Florida

Marineland is on Highway A1A between St. Augustine and Daytona Beach.

Marineland of Florida
9507 Ocean Shore Boulevard
Marineland, FL 32086
904-460-1275
Hours: Wednesday-Sunday, 9:30 A.M.-4:30 P.M.
Admission charged.

STATE FOLK FESTIVAL

Each Memorial Day weekend, the picturesque little northern Florida town of White Springs comes alive, as banjos, harmonicas, flutes, and fiddles fill the air with music. For three days and three nights, White Springs is host to the Florida Folk Festival, the country's first continuously running state folk festival.

In the early 1950s, members of the Florida Federation of Music Clubs conceived the idea of an annual festival that would be a celebration of

Florida's rich folk heritage, when Floridians and visitors alike could see and experience the state's cultural traditions. For ideas, they contacted such people as Alton Morris, editor of the journal *Southern Folklore Quarterly*, and Sarah Gertrude Knott, founder of the National Folk Festival, an annual event that took place in a different city each year to showcase the folk culture of the United States. In 1952, Knott came to Florida to see if it would be the right setting for this type of festival. She found a wealth of folklore and tradition and a huge pool of natural talent. Folk musicians, dancers, and storytellers could be found in all parts of the state. Knott organized and directed the first festival in 1953 and continues as director today.

First Festival

The first Florida Folk Festival was a rousing success, with more than 1,000 cars counted in the parking lot on the third and final day. All who participated agreed it should be a yearly event. Today it attracts more than 30,000 people from all over the United States and even from Latin America. The setting is the 850-acre Stephen Foster State Folk Culture Center on the banks of the Suwannee River. It is well known that Stephen Foster never saw the Suwannee but simply chose it from a map to use as the setting for his famous song "Old Folks at Home." However, this doesn't deter Floridians from claiming it as their state song and a deeply rooted part of their culture. Its strains are constantly heard throughout the festival.

Under a bigtop tent with a huge dance floor, line dancers, cloggers, and fans of blues, Latin, and jazz music can dance the night away. Workshops, concerts, and storytelling performances round out this joyous celebration of Florida's folk heritage.

☼ *To Visit: Florida Folk Festival*
The Florida Folk Festival runs for three days every Memorial Day weekend. To get to the festival, take Interstate 75 to the White Springs exit, 14 miles

north of Lake City. Follow the signs to the Stephen Foster State Folk Culture Center. For more information, call the festival information line, 904-488-1673.

CAGELESS ZOO

Back in the 1960s a group of European investors, noting that zoos in the United States kept their animals in cages, came up with the idea of creating a home for wild animals that would be modeled after African preserves, where the animals could roam free. In 1967, they opened Lion Country Safari near West Palm Beach, the nation's first cageless zoo.

Humans Confined

At Lion Country Safari it's the humans who must be confined, and what better "cage" than their own automobile? Of course, it can't be a convertible, and all windows must be in working order and kept rolled up. Air conditioning is virtually a necessity. But those who arrive with an unsuitable vehicle can rent a car from the park.

With strong warnings to keep doors fully closed and locked, visitors follow a road that leads through a 500-acre wildlife preserve. Animals have the right-of-way, so frequent stops are in order as an emu or a rhinoceros lumbers across the road. Over 1,000 exotic animals live here—gibbons, giraffes, elephants, zebras, and lions—in an environment created to be as similar as possible to their natural habitat.

Without the stress of being confined, the animals reproduce easily, as shown by the several generations of East African chimpanzees that live on five chimpanzee islands. Children especially like the petting zoo and the nursery, where they can watch newborn lion cubs and other baby animals.

Next to the preserve is an award-winning KOA campground, where campers can fall asleep to the sounds of nighttime Africa—lions roaring, gibbons whooping, cranes calling, and elephants trumpeting.

 **To Visit: Lion Country Safari**

Lion Country Safari is 18 miles west of West Palm Beach, off Southern Boulevard (State Road 90, 98, or 441).

Lion Country Safari

2003 Lion Country Safari Road
Loxahatchee, FL 33470
561-793-1084
Hours: Daily, 9:30 A.M.-5:30 P.M. (No vehicles admitted or tickets sold after 4:30 P.M.)
Admission charged.
The KOA campground next to Lion Country Safari has tents and rustic cabins for rent, as well as tent sites and full hook-up sites. For more information, call 561-793-9797.

GEODESIC SPHERE

Looking like an oversized golf ball, Spaceship Earth looms skyward at the entrance to Orlando's Epcot and dominates the entire park. The gigantic structure is a three-dimensional scale model of our planet, as close to accurate as the hand of man can make it. Almost completely spherical, only slightly less than perfect—steel supports throw off its dimensions just a bit—it is the first large-scale geodesic sphere in the world.

Other structures have been built to model the earth, but none was a true sphere. Montreal's Expo '77 sported a geodesic structure, but it was only partially spherical. And there have been geodesic domes; in fact, Spaceship Earth was originally planned to be the world's largest geodesic dome. In true Disney fashion, though, the larger vision prevailed. Planners wanted an entranceway that would make visitors shade their eyes, look upward, and say, "Wow!" The result is a geosphere 18 stories high, standing on six legs 18 feet off the ground, and weighing more than 5 million tons. It took 26 months to build.

Spaceship Earth is sponsored by the Bell System, and inside, the theme is man's communication through the ages. Seated in a "time machine," visitors travel upward through 40,000 years of recorded time, beginning with Stone Age man first learning to speak. The display then progresses to the development of alphabets, the first use of paper, writing, the invention of the printing press, and on to today's electronic communications and where we are headed in the future. Designers took care to make the displays as authentic as possible: in the ancient Egyptian scene, a pharaoh dictates an epistle to his scribe in a dialect that is amazingly accurate; an Islamic quadrant, an instrument used in navigation and astronomy, is a copy of one from the 10th century; Johann Gutenberg is depicted examining an exact replica of a page from an original Gutenberg Bible.

Spaceship Earth's exterior is made of 954 triangular panels with silvered facets that showcase the busy world around it. At night it reflects the stars and planets, as well as the World Showcase across the lagoon. Standing as a testament to man's creativity and ingenuity, it receives more visitors than any other attraction at Walt Disney World.

ALLIGATOR FARM

The St. Augustine Alligator Farm is one of the few tourist attractions listed on the National Register of Historic Places. It opened in 1893 as the first alligator farm in the nation. The farm, Florida's oldest continuously operating attraction, celebrated its centennial in 1993 with the grand opening of "Land of Crocodiles," the only exhibit in the world displaying all 23 species of crocodilians.

A Century in Business

In over a century of operation, the alligator farm has played a major role in the development of Florida's tourist industry. During its early days, when St. Augustine was a popular winter resort, many wealthy northerners put it on their list of places to see, along with the dungeons of Castillo de San Marcos and the quaint shops on St. George Street. After World War II, when it was visited by thousands of servicemen stationed at nearby Camp Blanding, its reputation spread across the nation.

Today, the attraction features alligator shows, which provide little-known facts about Florida's most dangerous animals; reptile shows, showcasing venomous and non-venomous snakes; and the Rainforest Review, featuring exotic parrots from South America in an entertaining and informative program about the world's vanishing rain forests. For the past three decades, the St. Augustine Alligator Farm has cooperated with scientists conducting research on the interactions of birds, reptiles, and other animals that live there.

☼ To Visit: St. Augustine Alligator Farm

St. Augustine Alligator Farm
999 Anastasia Boulevard
Anastasia Island
St. Augustine, FL 32084
904-824-3337
www.alligatorfarm.com
Hours: June-August: daily, 9 A.M.-6 P.M.; September-May: daily, 9 A.M.-5 P.M. Admission charged.

WATER-SKIING SHOW

While the sport of water-skiing actually began in the 1920s on a newly thawed lake in Minnesota, it was at Cypress Gardens near Winter Haven, Florida, that it first became an art form.

It was 1943, and while owner Dick Pope was serving in the army, his wife, Julie, had taken over operation of the popular tourist attraction. A group of airmen visiting from a nearby base had seen a picture taken at

Water-skiers form a pyramid at Cypress Gardens. *Courtesy of Cypress Gardens*

Cypress Gardens of skiers being towed behind boats. They asked Julie Pope when the ski show would start. She explained that the picture was an old one, distributed before her husband left to help in the war effort, and that the skiers in the picture were not performing, just having fun. "We don't have a show now," she said, and quickly added, "but we're going to." She told them to enjoy the gardens for a couple of hours and come back.

With the aid of her two teenagers and their friends, she arranged an impromptu water-skiing show. It was the first time anyone had ever used the sport for entertainment. The airmen liked it and told their friends, and the next weekend 800 airmen showed up. Julie knew she was on to something, and ran her family ski shows every week for the duration of World War II.

A water-skier performs a leap at Cypress Gardens. *Courtesy of Cypress Gardens*

Return from the War

When the war was over and Dick Pope returned, he used his promotional skills to turn the shows into a major attraction. He recruited and trained muscular young men to perform daredevil stunts that had never been attempted before. He took advantage of new technology to add style and pizzazz. He hired pretty young women, billed them as "Aquamaids," and trained them to do swivel stunts and water ballet. Without a large budget

---

CYPRESS GARDENS FIRSTS

Dick Pope is believed to be the first person to ski jump over a ramp in the water and the first to hang from a kite behind a boat. His son, Dick Jr., who was one of the performers in the first show and later became the owner of Cypress Gardens, was the first to water-ski barefoot.

---

for publicity, he arranged for Cypress Gardens' water-skiing shows to be featured in newsreels shown throughout the world.

Today, four shows daily feature holders of world ski-jumping records engaging in "aquabatics" that seem to defy the laws of gravity.

☀ To Visit: Cypress Gardens

Cypress Gardens
2641 South Lake Summit Drive
Winter Haven, FL 33884
863-324-2111
Hours: Vary; call for more information.
Admission charged.

ALL-BLACK CITY

Eatonville lies off Interstate 4, just 10 miles north of the heart of Orlando. Today it's a town of 2,500, with modest stucco, cinder-block, and wood-frame houses. Orange and grapefruit trees grow in the yards, along with pines, azaleas, and palmettos. The town has many of the problems that plague other small towns, such as the drug use and crime that filter in from the big cities. In many ways it's a typical small southern town of the new millennium, with one big difference: nearly all of its residents are black. Eatonville was founded on August 15, 1887, as the nation's first incorporated all-black town.

Three years earlier, most of Eatonville's residents had lived in nearby Maitland. Since Maitland needed 30 adult male voters in order to incorporate, blacks were encouraged to register and vote. They not only complied, they also outnumbered white voters and elected a black mayor and marshal. This was clearly not what the white Maitland residents had intended, so Captain Joshua Eaton and two other men offered to donate some land west of town and build a church and assembly hall for the blacks so they could found their own community.

Author Zora Neale Hurston was Eatonville's most famous native. *Courtesy of the Florida State Archives*

At first many of them hesitated. Released from slavery just two decades earlier, some were not sure they would be able to govern themselves. Others had more confidence, and the offer was accepted.

In many ways, life was good for the new residents. Plots of land were drawn large enough for each family to have a garden and grow its own vegetables. Since there was no division by color, prejudice didn't separate the residents. And to ensure that their children would get the education the older generation had been denied, the townspeople gave priority to establishing good schools.

A Famous Novelist

Eatonville's pride, novelist Zora Neale Hurston, was born there around the turn of the 20th century. Since her death in 1960, Hurston has been regarded as one of the century's leading black writers and experts on black folklore and culture. She wrote seven books, including the highly acclaimed *Their Eyes Were Watching God,* a novel about the hurricane of 1928 that killed thousands of farm workers living around Lake Okeechobee. In her autobiography, *Dust Tracks on a Road,* she describes the founding and growth of her hometown:

> So on August 18, 1886 [*sic*], the Negro town, called Eatonville, after Captain Eaton, received its charter of incorporation from the state capital, Tallahassee, and made history by becoming the first of its kind in America, and perhaps in the world. So, in a raw, bustling frontier, the experiment of self-government for Negroes was tried. White Maitland and Negro Eatonville have lived side by side for 56 years without a single instance of enmity. The spirit of the founders has reached beyond the grave.

Although Hurston traveled throughout the United States and to Haiti and the West Indies, it was from Eatonville that she drew most of her inspiration. The town figures prominently in her writings, and she recalls a happy, unhurried childhood. Today, a few residents remember her well, some fondly, others with misgivings at her openness in depicting her neighbors. Yet to honor her memory, the townspeople built the Zora Neale Hurston Museum of Fine Arts. Every winter the sleepy town awakens to honor its favorite daughter with the annual Zora Neale Hurston Festival

TRAGIC ENDING

Zora Neale Hurston spent her last days in poverty, working as a domestic servant in Fort Pierce. Several years after Hurston's death in 1960, Alice Walker, author of *The Color Purple,* placed on her unmarked grave a tombstone on which was inscribed "A genius of the South."

of the Arts and Humanities. The event includes a juried art show, music, dancing, storytelling, and mounds of southern soul food. One visitor wrote: "It is difficult to leave there not feeling full of heart and spirit."

☀ To Visit: Zora Neale Hurston Museum of Fine Arts

Zora Neale Hurston Museum of Fine Arts
227 East Kennedy Boulevard
Eatonville, FL 32751
407-647-3307

The Zora Neale Hurston Festival of the Arts and Humanities is held at East Kennedy Boulevard and College Avenue.
For dates and times, call 407-647-3307.

Firsts in Science, Medicine, and Government

GUIDED MISSILES

When Nazi Germany launched its V-2 guided missile against the Allies in World War II, it was a terrifying weapon, capable of destroying an entire city block. Fortunately, it wasn't used until the fall of 1944, too late in the war to save the Nazis. Few people at the time realized that unmanned flying bombs had actually had their beginnings shortly after World War I. The world's first guided missiles were launched on September 4, 1919, from Carlstrom Field in Arcadia, a cattle town in central Florida.

The first tests were an embarrassment to the top military brass who gathered in Arcadia to watch them. In one test, a torpedo fell off at 200 feet and crashed. Another torpedo had motor failure at $1^3/_4$ miles. When still another reached 2 miles, its wings fell off. The last torpedo reached 16 miles, on course, but crashed due to motor failure.

Because it would have taken too much time and money to perfect the missiles, the Allies never used them as weapons in World War II. The research that went into making them, however, was invaluable later in the development of missile technology and manned exploration of space.

HEALTH MAINTENANCE ORGANIZATION

In 1888, Don Enrique Pendas, a Spanish tobacco worker in Ybor City, saw a need for health insurance in the newly established cigar industry. On June 18 of that year, he organized El Porvenir, the country's first health maintenance organization.

In return for small weekly dues, the Spanish, Italian, and Cuban workers received medicine as well as hospitalization and medical services. The system worked well, and soon each nationality established its own group. El Porvenir was followed in 1891 by El Centro Español, in 1894 by L'Unione Italiana, and in 1902 by El Círculo Cubano and El Centro Asturiano.

There was no sense of competition among the groups, and they cooperated nicely. Tuberculosis and yellow fever were constant threats, and the organizations worked together to build clinics and two hospitals and to hire trained medical personnel. These early HMOs helped the proud group of immigrants remain independent. A marker near an early cigar factory in Ybor City states that the cigar workers "have never been a burden on society, and through the years have saved tax-payers millions of dollars."

Unfortunately, envious Tampa physicians were opposed to the idea of the cigar workers and their families getting the best medical care at very low cost. The county medical society barred the Ybor City physicians and nurses from practicing in the city's hospitals. Eventually the HMOs bowed to the more powerful group and were forced to disband.

DISCOVERER OF THE CAUSE OF YELLOW FEVER

While Dr. Walter Reed and his U.S. Army Commission in 1900 took most of the credit for discovering the cause of yellow fever, it actually had been identified 27 years earlier by a Tampa physician, Dr. John Perry Wall.

For centuries, the dreaded disease had caused epidemics and panics the world over, once even halting construction of the Panama Canal. The Florida coast was one of the places hit hardest by the scourge. In the mid-1800s, it was widely believed that poor sanitary conditions were the cause of the disease. But massive efforts to rid lawns, barnyards, streets, and outhouses of dirt and fecal matter brought no relief. Another theory was that the disease came from vapors given off by dank wetlands. Smoking tar barrels were lit to eliminate them. Still the fever raged unchecked.

A Personal Tragedy

Wall had a personal interest in solving the mystery. When yellow fever first broke out in Tampa in 1871, a cabin boy on a ship in the port came down with it. After treating the boy and restoring him to health, Wall contracted the disease. His young wife nursed him, but he had barely recovered when she and their two-year-old daughter caught it and died. The grief-stricken doctor resolved to do everything in his power to find the cause of the disease and eliminate it.

After much study and research, Wall became convinced that the treetop mosquito was the real cause of yellow fever. He observed that both the mosquito and the fever appeared only in the summer months. He also noted that the disease occurred mostly in people who had some reason to go outside at night, when the insect was most prevalent. But in 1873, when Wall proposed the idea that a mosquito could be the cause of yellow fever, no one took him seriously. The theory that unsanitary conditions caused the disease continued to prevail.

Proof of the Theory

It was not until 1900, five years after Wall's death, that Dr. Reed and his commission proved the treetop mosquito to be the culprit. When the researchers isolated the insect and let it bite volunteers, the evidence was conclusive. But proving the cause of yellow fever had a high price: a volunteer doctor caught the disease and almost died, and a scientist was accidentally bitten and died a few days later.

OTHER CONTRIBUTIONS
Dr. John Wall served as mayor of Tampa, first president of the Tampa Board of Trade, and president of the state medical association.

CONTACT LENS IMPLANTED

On March 5, 1997, Dr. David C. Brown successfully completed the nation's first implantable–contact lens procedure. This was a medical breakthrough for the permanent correction of nearsightedness and farsightedness.

Brown, founder and medical director of Eye Centers of Florida in Fort Myers, was one of four ophthalmologists chosen to participate in a multiphase clinical study to investigate the implantable contact lens (ICL). The study was sponsored by STAAR Surgical Company of Monrovia, California, which had successfully introduced a foldable-lens implant for cataract surgery in 1984. Brown was one of the first surgeons in Florida to test the STAAR foldable lens and to use "no-stitch" cataract surgery.

The Old and the New

Brown explained the difference between cataract surgery and the new procedure, which uses the implantable lens: "Unlike excimer-laser surgery, in which the cornea is reshaped, the patient's eye is not surgically altered [when the implantable contact lens is used]. The natural crystalline lens, [which is] removed during cataract surgery, remains in place. The ICL is placed between the natural crystalline lens and the iris." The surgeon positions the ICL through a closed, sterile pathway created by making a tiny incision in the cornea. Patients heal much faster than they would after cataract surgery.

Despite the initial favorable results of this operation, it won't be available for a few years. STAAR is running extensive tests to determine the long-term outcome of the procedure before offering it to the general public.

MINIMALLY INVASIVE HEART-VALVE SURGERY

On March 14, 1996, Dr. Carl C. Gill performed the first minimally invasive heart-valve surgery at the Cleveland Clinic Florida in Fort Lauderdale. Performed through a three-inch incision, the operation is much less painful and much easier to tolerate than standard open-heart surgery.

Gill learned the technique at the Cleveland Clinic Foundation, where it was developed by Delos M. Cosgrove III, M.D., early in 1996. As with traditional open-heart surgery, the heart is stopped during the operation as the patient is placed on cardiopulmonary bypass. But the new surgery does not require the chest to be split open. The heart is exposed by removing two small pieces of cartilage.

"It is an excellent approach because patients do not require so much pain medication and can get back on their feet quickly," Dr. Gill explained. Patients can walk the day after surgery and are usually discharged three days later. However, this method of treatment may not be readily available to all who need it. It is a highly specialized technique, and although it is much easier on the patient than the traditional surgery, it requires greater technical skill on the part of the surgeon.

FEMALE ATTORNEY GENERAL

When Janet Reno was sworn in on March 12, 1993, as the 78th attorney general of the United States, critics argued that no woman could be tough-minded enough for the job. In an office plagued with controversy from the beginning, Reno quietly proved them wrong.

Janet Reno, former U.S. attorney general. *Courtesy of the Florida State Archives*

She had already proved herself in her hometown of Miami. Thirty years earlier, when she returned there armed with a law degree from Harvard, female lawyers were rare, and finding a job was not easy. One of the city's most prestigious law firms turned her down. Fourteen years later, it made her a partner.

Reno was elected state attorney for Dade County and was reelected four times. Her office encompassed the entire Greater Miami area and had 940 employees, a $30 million annual budget, and a yearly docket of 120,000 cases.

Early Life

Reno was born in Miami in 1938 to two newspaper reporters. Her mother, Jane Wood Reno, once wrestled alligators, interviewed gangsters, and built the family home in South Miami with her own hands. Jane Reno died in 1992, just a few months after Hurricane Andrew proved the durability of the house she had built 46 years earlier. Only one shingle and a few screens were lost. Her death, however, came three months before what surely would have been one of her proudest moments, the inauguration of her daughter as attorney general of the United States.

Controversy

Although Reno was President Bill Clinton's third choice for attorney general, she took the nation's capital by storm when she arrived. "Reno is pure oxygen in a city with thin air," reported *Time* magazine in its July 12, 1993, issue, and "Clinton's most impressive cabinet member by far." She was commended for her strength and integrity and was highly praised for bringing those qualities into the Justice Department.

Her tenure, however, seemed to start off on the wrong foot. Only a month after taking office, she ordered a raid on the Branch Davidian cult compound in Waco, Texas, which left at least 75 people dead. A few years later her popularity, as well as her reputation for integrity, diminished in the wake of some decisions that failed to find favor with a growing

MORE CONTROVERSY

Attorney General Janet Reno took one of the most controversial actions of her career in 2000 when she ordered an armed raid by the Immigration and Naturalization Service to take six-year-old Elian Gonzalez from the home of his Miami relatives and return him to his Cuban father. Elian's great-uncle had been fighting for custody of the child since he was found floating off the Florida coast, holding onto an inner tube, after his mother drowned while bringing him to the United States from Cuba.

number of people, especially certain Capitol Hill Republicans. In 1998, she antagonized many for failing to take the advice of top investigators in a campaign-finance scandal. A year later, she was criticized for her failure to act in a serious Chinese espionage case and for granting lenient plea bargains to the two principals. Angry Republicans called for her resignation.

But Reno weathered the criticism with her characteristic tough-mindedness and refused to accommodate anyone by resigning. Now, out of office since Bill Clinton left the White House, she continues to champion her favorite causes, especially prevention and early intervention to keep children away from gangs, drugs, and violence.

STATE TO DELAY A PRESIDENTIAL ELECTION

Florida's latest first is one for the history books and one that every American hopes will be a "last." For 36 days after voters went to the polls on November 7, 2000, in the presidential race between Texas governor George W. Bush and Vice President Al Gore, the outcome was uncertain. And it was Florida that was holding it up.

For weeks before the first vote was cast, political experts were predicting that the winner of Florida's 25 electoral votes would be the next U.S. president. The race was going to be close. While other key states leaned strongly toward one candidate or the other, the outcome in Florida was impossible to predict.

At 7 P.M. on Election Day, television networks projected Gore the winner in Florida, only to retract the projection when later returns came in. In the early-morning hours of November 8, they declared Bush the winner in Florida, and the nation, by a very slim margin. Gore called him and conceded, but retracted his concession upon learning that Florida law calls for an automatic recount when vote totals are within half a percent.

What followed was a month of turmoil and confusion. Gore's lawyers pushed for hand recounts in several counties. Bush's lawyers made every attempt to stop such recounts. In the Electoral College, Gore held 267 electoral votes and Bush had 246 of the 270 needed to win the presidency. Florida's electoral votes—which would go to the candidate who won the state's popular vote—would make all the difference.

Numerous important questions arose: Which ballots should be counted? Absentee ballots that had come in after the deadline? "Dimpled" punch-card ballots, in which the pin had not gone completely through the card? Then there was the problem of chads, the part of the ballot that was punched out: voting machines sometimes forced the chads back in and counted the ballot as a non-vote. What about the ballots in heavily Democratic Palm Beach County, where many voters claimed a new ballot design had led them to vote for Reform Party candidate Pat Buchanan when they intended to vote for Gore? Angry voters demanded—but were never granted—a revote.

And what about the recounts themselves? Were they required? Were they legal? Were they accurate and fair? With no precedent for this sort of thing, there were no clear answers. Democrats answered yes to all the questions; Republicans said no.

With recounts being started, then halted, time and again, it soon became clear that this was an election where the will of the voters could never be known for certain. On November 26, Florida's secretary of state, Katherine Harris, declared Bush the winner by 537 popular votes. But even as the governor was planning his move to the White House, Gore contested the results in three counties. Both candidates filed briefs with the United States Supreme Court. Two more weeks of trials and appeals followed.

Finally, on December 12, a divided U.S. Supreme Court ruled against any more recounts, assuring a victory for Bush. The next day, Gore conceded the election. And on December 18, the Electoral College officially secured Bush's position as the president-elect.

The historic hold-up made one thing clear: the process of electing a United States president is badly flawed, with horse-and-buggy equipment, outdated laws, and inconsistencies among the states. Investigations showed that ballots could still be stolen or bought, that vote-counting machines could be woefully inaccurate, that there is no clear procedure to follow in an election this close. Events in Florida have led many Americans to question how we elect someone to the highest office in the land.

COUNTY TO USE METROPOLITAN GOVERNMENT

In 1957, Miami–Dade County became the first area in the country to successfully use metropolitan government. The system, which coordinates city and county government into one centralized unit, was designed to minimize political conflict and prevent many of the problems that often arise from unchecked urban growth.

The city of Miami had been in financial difficulty since the collapse of the 1920s land boom, followed by the Great Depression, and had been forced to cut back services and de-annex some territory. With the area's spectacular growth in the 1940s and 1950s, the city government found it increasingly difficult to cope with the needs for hospitals, new bridges and water tunnels, fire and police protection, slum clearance, and public transportation and parking. With 26 separate municipalities in Dade County, as well as a huge unincorporated area, these services were fragmented and costly. Political reformers began to realize that consolidation of services would be the only way to put Miami and Dade County on solid financial footing.

Growth of the Plan

In 1953, after several failed attempts to pass legislation that would bring "Metro" government to the county, the Miami City Commission formed the Metropolitan Miami Municipal Board to study the feasibility of consolidation. The board hired a Chicago consulting firm, which recommended a structured government in which the municipalities would retain certain local services and the county would take over functions such as mass transit, planning, water, and sewage. In May 1957, voters approved the plan.

Under the Miami-Dade plan, cities and special districts remain intact, with their own governing bodies. Each has its own charter, which identifies and defines its special functions. The governments are organized to work closely together, with the county acting as local coordinator. It is the county, rather than the state, that governs and serves unincorporated areas. This provides for a more equitable tax structure and better services for these areas.

Structured Government

Miami–Dade County is governed by the Board of County Commissioners, which is made up of commissioners elected from each of the 13 districts of the county and the mayor, whose main function is to preside at commission meetings. An appointed county manager, a highly trained and experienced professional aided by a professional staff, performs the executive functions of Metro. Thus, problems are resolved at the administrative level, rather than at the political level.

Metro government may not be for everybody. In areas where citizens have lived for generations and retain strong loyalties to their cities, people may not like the idea of a centralized government. But for those regions where rapid growth is a problem and cities are overrunning their boundaries, it seems a logical alternative. It has worked well in Miami, and other cities with similar problems, such as Jacksonville and Denver, Colorado, have adopted it.

Lady Racers and Record Setters

FIRST LADY OF AVIATION AND AUTOMOBILE FIRSTS

Floridian Betty Skelton Frankman has set more records in the combined fields of aviation and automobile racing than any other person. In 1938, when she was 12 years old, she flew a plane solo—making her, at that time, the youngest person to accomplish such a feat. Until 1965, when she raced a jet car on the Salt Flats of Bonneville, Utah, to become the first woman to reach a speed of over 300 miles per hour in an automobile, she continued to accumulate firsts. She was the first woman in the world to:

★ Receive a race driver's AAA license (1954)

★ Drive an Indianapolis racecar (1954)

★ Establish NASCAR records at Daytona Beach (1954)

★ Win the Feminine International Aerobatic Championship three times

★ Break the world land speed record for women four times

★ Become a test driver in the auto industry (1954–55)

★ Become a member of the International Aerobatic Club Hall of Fame

★ Become a member of the NASCAR International Automotive Hall of Fame

Betty Skelton flies over Tampa in her Pitts Special biplane, *The Little Stinker,* in 1951. *Courtesy of Betty Skelton Frankman*

Early Life

Born in Pensacola in 1926, Frankman learned to fly at her father's aviation school at Peter O. Knight Airport in Tampa. Soon after she received her pilot's license from the Civil Aeronautics Administration (CAA) on her 16th birthday, she began winning aerobatic championships and setting air records. She became a test pilot and flew helicopters, jets, blimps, and gliders.

First Airplane

In 1948, she purchased her first plane, a Serial #1 Pitts Special experimental biplane, with one seat and an open cockpit. At 544 pounds, it was at that time the smallest plane in the world. Despite being equipped with a smoke-dispensing apparatus that caused some unsavory odors to fill the cockpit, the tiny plane seemed perfect for its 98-pound owner. She named it *The Little Stinker,* and it soon became the world's most famous aerobatic aircraft. When Frankman flew from Liverpool, England, to Belfast, Northern Ireland, her plane was the smallest ever to cross the Irish Sea. And it was in *The Little Stinker* that she enthralled audiences with her famous stunt of flying upside down 10 feet above the ground to cut a ribbon with her wing tip.

In the early 1950s, feeling restricted by gender barriers in aviation, Frankman retired from professional flying and turned to automobiles for more challenges. She began setting speed records at Daytona and on the Chrysler Proving Grounds. The Dodge division of the Chrysler Corporation hired her as the first woman automobile test driver in the industry. In 1956, she became an advertising executive for the Campbell-Ewald Company in Detroit and worked there for 15 years. In 1965, she married Donald Frankman, and the two later moved to Winter Haven, Florida, where they established First Florida Realty.

On March 15, 1997, Betty Skelton Frankman was enshrined in the International Pioneer Aviation Hall of Fame in Dallas, Texas. She plans to write a book about the importance of accepting challenges. "I still love fast cars," she said recently, "and would welcome another opportunity to top my old women's record." Her first plane, *The Little Stinker,* built in 1946, has been fully restored and now hangs in the National Air and Space Museum of the Smithsonian Institution in Washington, D.C.

LADY ROAD RACE WINNER

In 1985, at Watkins Glen, New York, Lyn St. James of Daytona Beach became the first woman to win a professional road race driving solo. Later that year, when she reached 204.233 miles per hour in a Ford Mustang prototype, she became the first woman to drive faster than 200 miles per hour on an oval track.

In 1984, St. James was named the IMSA Camel GT Rookie of the Year, and in 1985 she was chosen as the IMSA Norelco Driver of the Year. She was a winning GTO team member at the 24 Hours of Daytona in 1987 and 1990 and at the 12 Hours of Sebring in 1991. She began competing in the Indianapolis 500 in 1992, when she was named rookie of the year, and participated in that race for three more years. In 1993, she established the Lyn St. James Foundation, which promotes automotive safety and driver development, especially for women who aspire to be racecar drivers.

WOMAN TO BREAK SOUND BARRIER

She was born around 1906 in the little Florida sawmill town of Muskogee and learned to read by figuring out the letters on the railroad boxcars that went by. She had no shoes until she was eight years old, and home was

Jacqueline Cochran meets President Dwight D. Eisenhower. *Courtesy of the Florida State Archives*

UNSOLVED MYSTERY

In her autobiography, *Stars at Noon*, Jacqueline Cochran states that she was a foster child and never learned the circumstances of her birth, not even the date it occurred. After her death, relatives claimed that Cochran, who changed her name from Pittman, had a flair for the dramatic, that she was born on May 11, 1906, and that she grew up with her own biological parents and siblings. We may never know the truth.

usually a "shack on stilts." It seemed unlikely that Jacqueline Cochran would one day be known as one of the world's most famous women fliers and test pilots and head of the Women's Airforce Service Pilots (WASP) in World War II. On May 18, 1953, while piloting an F-86 Sabre at 625.5 miles per hour, she became the first woman to break the sound barrier.

Cochran was introduced to flying in 1932 by millionaire Floyd Odlum, who later became her husband. She soloed three days after her first lesson and earned her pilot's license in three weeks. One of her early feats led to mandatory pressurized cabins and oxygen masks: she flew a biplane to 33,000 feet without heat, pressure, or an oxygen mask and almost met her death, which could easily have come by freezing or by fainting from lack of oxygen and crashing. In 1971, she became the first woman to be enshrined in the National Aviation Hall of Fame in Dayton, Ohio. She died in 1980.

FEMALE JOCKEY

When Diane Crump raced her horse, Fathom, at Hialeah Park on February 7, 1969, she was the first female jockey to compete against men in a sanctioned race. With 50-to-1 odds, she finished 10th in the race.

WOMAN TO SAIL SOLO ACROSS THE ATLANTIC

When Ann Davidson docked her 23-foot sailboat, the *Felicity Ann*, in Miami on August 12, 1953, she became the first woman to cross the Atlantic Ocean alone in a sailboat. Her trip had begun on May 18, 1952, in Plymouth, England.

The following year, Crump became the first woman to ride in the Kentucky Derby. While others soon followed her example at Hialeah, it would be 14 years before another woman would ride in the derby.

Horse Trainer

Crump stopped riding in 1984, and in 1990 got her trainer's license. She excelled in the field of horse training—breaking yearlings and getting thoroughbreds ready to race. Her horses raced in Maryland, Delaware, West Virginia, and Pennsylvania. One of her most notable products was three-year-old filly champion Saratoga Dew.

In 1991, Crump decided to ride again and entered a race at Turfway in Kentucky, riding Punch It Margaret, a horse she had trained. She is one of the few people—male or female—who have ever been a jockey and a trainer at the same time.

WINNER OF WORLD RECORDS IN BOTH SWIMMING AND DIVING

In the 1930s, Katherine "Katy" Rawls, winner of a record 30 national titles, was the one to beat in swimming and diving. The first athlete to win world records in both sports, she captured 14 national outdoor swimming titles, 11 national indoor swimming titles, and 5 national diving titles. In national

Katherine Rawls accepts congratulations from a foreign dignitary after a meet.
Courtesy of the Fort Lauderdale Historical Society

competition in 1933, the year she moved to Fort Lauderdale, she won the 200-meter breaststroke, the half-mile freestyle, the 300-meter individual medley, and the springboard diving championship. During a nine-year career, from 1930 to 1939, she won more national championships than any other woman.

A Charmer

Rawls's personality and charm endeared her to the public. Featured in newsreels and newspapers, she helped sell southern Florida to the world. In 1939, disappointed that the 1940 Olympic Games were to be canceled due to war in Europe, she retired from water sports. After taking up flying and marrying her flight instructor, Ted Thompson, she became one of the world's top women fliers and helped found the Women's Airforce Service Pilots, or WASP. She was selected for the U.S. Women's Auxiliary Ferrying Squadron to shuttle World War II planes to combat zones.

Since Rawls was a hometown girl, the residents of Fort Lauderdale felt it only fitting that the International Swimming Hall of Fame be located in their city. In 1965, Rawls officially opened the new Hall of Fame swimming pool and was one of the first group of 21 inductees.

SWIMMER TO CROSS LAKE ONTARIO FROM NORTH TO SOUTH

On August 31, 1974, 25-year-old Diana Nyad became the first swimmer to make the difficult north-to-south crossing of Lake Ontario. She also attempted to make the return trip, but was pulled from the water, unconscious, after swimming 20 hours and 30 minutes and completing about 37 miles of the 64-mile round trip. The year before, when she won a 26-mile race in Argentina's Paraná River, Nyad had set the women's world record for long-distance swimming. She also completed a swim of 22 miles from Capri to Naples, Italy, and another around Manhattan Island.

Nyad began swimming when she was six months old and started training seriously at the age of 11. In 1970, she began training for marathon swimming. She states in her autobiography, *Other Shores,* that by her own choice, her childhood in Fort Lauderdale consisted of rigorous training sessions. With a heart and mind dedicated to becoming the best swimmer in the world, she had no interest in the usual childhood activities.

In 1978, Nyad attempted her most ambitious project of all, a 103-mile swim from Marathon, Florida, to Havana, Cuba, ensconced in a motorized cage to ward off sharks. The cage, however, took on water and produced waves that caused Nyad to become nauseated. The six-foot waves outside the cage were also much higher than she had anticipated. Nyad was forced to stop a few miles short of the finish.

In 1979, Nyad swam her last marathon, 89 miles from the Bahamas to Florida, in 27 hours and 38 minutes. She later became a sports commentator for ABC-TV.

Sports in the Sun

GOLF COURSE

When Scots settled Sarasota, they brought their favorite game. J. Hamilton Gillespie, the city's first mayor, built the nation's first golf course there in 1886.

Gillespie's father, Sir John Gillespie, was president of a Scottish syndicate that purchased 60,000 acres of Florida land, including the site of present-day Sarasota. He sent his son to inspect the land, which had long been used by sportsmen for tarpon fishing and kingfishing. Young Gillespie built a rustic hotel to accommodate the fishermen and laid out a small golf course.

Gillespie's course had only four holes, but it sparked Floridians' interest in the game. Soon every first-class resort in the state had to have at least one golf course. Gillespie established courses in several other Florida cities, including Jacksonville and Tampa, and one in Havana, Cuba. He stayed in Sarasota and remained an avid golfer for the rest of his life. On September 7, 1923, while playing golf on his course, he suffered a heart attack and died a few hours later.

By 1890, golf had caught on in the eastern United States, and posh country clubs from Florida to New England were building elegant, professionally designed courses for their wealthy clientele. Nobody knows when it happened, but the small course in what is now downtown Sarasota was plowed under and

---

LEADER IN GOLF COURSES

Today, Florida leads the nation in the number of golf courses with 1,120. California, in second place, has 898.

---

forgotten. For decades, tourists and busy Sarasotans passed the site daily, unaware of its historical significance.

Renewed Interest

Interest has been revived in recent years, however. In 1999, construction began on the site, now known as Links Plaza, for a modern business complex, with two restaurants and a bank. A small public park now features a sculpture of a golfer with two fountains. "It's fascinating to observe," said Sarasota's former mayor, Mollie Cardamone, who came up with the idea of the fountain when she saw a similar one at Disney's Epcot in Orlando. "It makes the park not only a commemoration of Hamilton Gillespie but a place that people are going to want to come to."

NBA ROOKIE PLAYER OF THE WEEK

In his first year as an NBA player, basketball star Shaquille O'Neal became the first rookie since Michael Jordan to be named as a starter in the NBA All-Star Game. At the age of 20, he was the youngest player ever to participate in this event. But his most amazing feat was being named player of the week during his very first week in the NBA, making him the first player to receive this honor as a rookie.

MORE MOOLA

Shaquille O'Neal has made two rap albums and two singles and has appeared in two motion pictures. He has done a commercial for Taco Bell and endorsed products for Reebok, Pepsi-Cola, Spalding, and other companies. His net worth today is more than $70 million.

This achievement was the first of many. During his rookie year, after signing with the Orlando Magic as the number-one pick in the 1992 NBA draft, Shaq averaged 23 points and 14 rebounds per game. His contract called for a record $40 million over seven years. In 1996, he signed a seven-year, $123 million contract with the Los Angeles Lakers. He was named one of the 50 greatest players in NBA history, the youngest player ever to receive this honor. Even though he now plays for the Lakers, Shaq maintains his $3 million, 20,000-square-foot mansion in the Orlando suburb of Windemere.

MAJOR AUTO RACETRACK

Almost as soon as the first automobiles were produced, adventurous souls began to think about racing them. A few races were held in the New York, Chicago, and Boston areas, but the tracks caused problems. Dust and dirt stirred up by cars made driving at high speeds pretty unpleasant.

With its luxurious Ormond Hotel, Ormond Beach at the turn of the century had become a playground for the rich, many of whom were fascinated by the newfangled "horseless carriage." The hotel fronted on a 23-mile stretch of smooth sand that had been used for several years for racing bicycles. In 1902, when J. F. Hathaway, a guest at the hotel, noticed that his bicycle tires barely left an imprint, he drove his Stanley Steamer

Drivers line up for a race on the sand in Ormond Beach. *Courtesy of the Florida State Archives*

over the track and discovered it could support an automobile. The sand, packed hard by pounding waves and baked by the Florida sun, remained firmly in place. It was a perfect surface for the world's first major auto-racing track.

Racing on the Sand

Word got out to two other hotel guests, both automobile manufacturers, who decided to race in their own cars. Ransome E. Olds, who the year before had introduced America's first mass-produced car, the Curved-Dash Oldsmobile, would race Alexander Winton. Olds's car, the "Pirate," had a one-cylinder, water-cooled engine, while Winton drove "Bullet #1," which sported wooden wheels and was cooled by a front-end radiator. The race was declared a tie, with both cars clocked at a phenomenal 57 miles per hour.

FIRST 500

Race driver Lee Petty had to wait three days to find out that he was the winner of the first Daytona 500. The race was so close between Petty and Johnny Beauchamp that officials had to carefully study a photograph of the finish.

Later, a racing course was designed that reached 25 miles down the beach from Ormond and entered Daytona Beach. Car racing on the sand continued until 1935, when Sir Malcolm Campbell shattered a world record in his new Bluebird, which boasted a 2,500-horsepower Rolls Royce engine. His speed of 278.816 miles per hour was considered too fast for safety. It was the last race on the Ormond–Daytona track.

In the 1950s, construction began on the Daytona International Speedway, a modern, $2^1/_2$-mile, oval-shaped auto racetrack. The first Daytona 500 was held in 1959, and Daytona Beach became the racing capital of the world.

THREE-TIME WINNER OF MAJOR GOLF TITLES

It was 1971, and golfer Jack Nicklaus's game at the PGA tournament in Palm Beach Gardens had been off. The first day out, he ended up in the sand four times. But by the end of the tournament he had managed to pull his game together and win the coveted trophy. As fellow golfer Bob Hope presented it to him, Nicklaus was hailed as the first two-time winner in history of each of the "Big Four" of golf—the Masters, the U.S. Open, the British Open, and the PGA Championship. Not one to rest on his laurels, Nicklaus went on later in his career to win each Big Four tournament a third time.

Jack Nicklaus (right) talks with touring pro Dow Finsterwald before the $2,000 Pensacola Open in 1962. *Courtesy of the Florida State Archives*

Nicklaus was born in Columbus, Ohio, in 1940 and began playing golf at the age of 10. After winning his first major tournament, the Ohio Open, at 16, he went on to win major amateur and college championships. As a professional, he continued this outstanding record and won the PGA's Golfer of the Century award in 1988. He joined the senior tour in 1990 and won the U.S. Senior Open twice.

The Golden Bear

Dubbed the "Golden Bear," Nicklaus made Florida his permanent home when he moved to Riviera Beach in 1970. He became a manufacturer of golfing equipment and a designer of championship golf courses.

Nicklaus, a father of five and now a grandfather, gives much of the credit for his success to a stable and happy home life. He has said many times that golf is "just a game" and takes second billing to his family. He seems undaunted by the prospect that a young golf genius named Tiger Woods appears destined to claim his unofficial title as the best golfer ever.

WOMAN TO WIN $1 MILLION IN TENNIS

In 1976, after only four years as a professional, Christine Marie Evert became the first female tennis player in history to win $1 million.

Born in Fort Lauderdale in 1954, Evert began playing tennis at the age of 6. She was coached by her father, Jimmy Evert, head pro at the city's

Chris Evert displays her famous two-handed backhand. *Courtesy of the Florida State Archives*

CHRIS EVERT CHARITIES

In 1989, Chris Evert founded Chris Evert Charities. Not content to just lend her name, she has been an active member of the board of directors. The organization has raised more than $7 million to fight drug abuse in southern Florida and to give at-risk infants a second chance at life.

Holiday Park. As a ponytailed youngster with a lightning-fast, two-handed backhand, Chrissie, as she was known to family and friends, was a familiar sight at the park, thriving on long, arduous practice sessions. From an early age she showed the concentration and mental toughness that would make her the world's number-one woman player eight times. She came up through the ranks of junior tournament tennis and from the age of 10 was always number one in her age group.

The world first noticed Evert in 1970 when, at the age of 15, she beat 28-year-old Margaret Court, the player ranked number one in the world. The following year, she became the youngest player to reach the semifinals of the U.S. Open. Since her parents insisted she finish high school before turning professional, she had to turn down more than $50,000 in prize money before 1972.

A Great Career

Evert's phenomenal career included 157 singles titles, 18 in Grand Slam events, which set a record for both men and women players. She became the first player to win at least one Grand Slam title for 13 consecutive years. Between 1973 and 1979, she won a record 125 consecutive clay-court matches. She won the U.S. Open six times and Wimbledon three times. In 1995, she was inducted into the International Tennis Hall of

Fame in Newport, Rhode Island, with former president George Bush doing the honors.

Evert retired from circuit play in 1988, but played on her country's team for the Federation Cup, the world's premier international women's team tennis competition. She won five matches and brought another Federation Cup to the United States. She now lives with her husband, Andy Mill, and three sons in Boca Raton.

JAI ALAI FRONTON

Jai alai (pronounced *high lie*) is an exciting but dangerous game played on a three-walled *cancha*, or court, with a small, hard ball. It is one of the oldest ball games in the world, dating back to the 15th century in the Pyrenees in Spain, when one of the first players decided to use a breadbasket to throw and retrieve a ball. Today, a long, curved wicker basket called a *cesta* is fitted with a glove and strapped to each player's hand. The object is to

A new Biscayne Fronton opened after the first one was destroyed in the 1926 hurricane. *Courtesy of the Florida State Archives*

DESI'S FIRST JOB

Desi Arnaz, later married to Lucille Ball and star of TV's *I Love Lucy*, had his first job in the United States at the Biscayne Fronton, singing for fans between games.

hurl the ball against the walls hard enough that the other player will miss it or commit a foul. Each game lasts about 15 minutes, and 14 games are played in an evening. Many players come from the Basque region of Spain.

In 1924, after Florida passed a state law permitting pari-mutuel betting on jai alai, the first fronton, or jai alai arena, in the United States was built in Miami. Destroyed by the 1926 hurricane, the Biscayne Fronton was rebuilt in 1928. Today there are several other jai alai frontons in Florida, as well as arenas in Connecticut, Rhode Island, and Nevada.

COACH TO USE SPLIT-LINE T FORMATION

The Split-Line T formation, now used by nearly every college and professional football team in the nation, was introduced in 1956 by Alonzo S. "Jake" Gaither, then head football coach and athletic director at Florida A&M University (FAMU) in Tallahassee.

A WINNER

Jake Gaither, often called "the winningest coach in football," coined the slogan "I like my boys agile, mobile, and hostile."

Florida A&M football coach Jake Gaither leads his team in a pre-game prayer. *Courtesy of the Florida State Archives*

"Coach Jake Gaither has proven to be an offensive genius. His Split-Line T has brought a new dimension to football," said Woody Hayes, head football coach of Ohio State University. This was strong praise for the coach of what was then a small African American college in the segregated South.

Gaither spread his offensive linemen over a distance about 15 feet wider than the 33 feet used in the regular T formation. This gave the offense more control over the positions of the players and provided better blocking angles. From 1956 to 1962, FAMU won 62 games and lost 5 using the Split-Line T.

Gaither retired from coaching after the 1969 season with a record of 203 wins, 36 losses, and 4 ties. In 1975, he was inducted into the National Football Foundation's hall of fame. He died in 1994, at the age of 90.

RACEHORSE TO WIN AN ACCOLADE FROM A UNIVERSITY

In January 1956, when the Letterman's Club of Oklahoma A&M University inducted a new member, it was the first time such a distinction had been bestowed upon a horse. But this wasn't just any horse. Needles was a champion thoroughbred, born and raised in Ocala, Florida, and the winner of unprecedented honors. Oklahoma A&M was the alma mater of his owner, Bonnie Heath.

Nothing about Needles's early life indicated the heights he would achieve. As a five-week-old colt he contracted equine pneumonia, a disease that is often fatal. His trainer, Roy Yates, worked around the clock with a veterinarian and a trained nurse, administering oxygen to save his life. They also gave him numerous injections, earning him the name "Needles."

A Champion

Needles was about 18 months old before he began to show the promise that would make him a champion. As a precocious two-year-old, he began his career on March 29, 1955, at Gulfstream Park in Hollywood, Florida. He won his first start by five lengths, missing the track record by two-fifths of a length.

On October 15, Needles won the Garden State Stakes at Monmouth Park, New Jersey, setting a track record of $1:37^{1}/_{5}$ for the mile. He finished the season with six wins, two third-place finishes, and earnings of $129,805. When he was voted the champion two-year-old of 1955, he became Florida's first national champion.

High-Spirited

Needles proved to be a spirited horse, with a mind of his own. He balked at morning workouts and frequently showed a nasty temper. But the public loved him, and Bonnie Heath said he had never seen a horse with more heart and courage. In 1956, he entered Needles in the most prestigious competition in the United States, the Kentucky Derby.

Whether Needles's high-spiritedness would be a handicap or a blessing remained to be seen, until he won the Kentucky Derby and changed the reputation of Florida horse breeding forever. For the first time, racing fans throughout the world realized that the Sunshine State could hold its own with Kentucky as a breeder of fine horses.

SHUFFLEBOARD ON LAND

While the origins of shuffleboard go back to the 1400s, it was first played as a table game. Later, sailors adapted it as a deck game on ships. It was not until 1913 that Robert Ball built the first shuffleboard court on land at a hotel he owned in Daytona Beach. Ball and his wife had learned the game while on an ocean cruise ship.

Later, two courts were built in St. Petersburg, where a shuffleboard club was formed in 1924. In 1928, enthusiasts of the game created the Florida Shuffleboard Association. In 1958, a national shuffleboard association was organized.

SHUFFLEBOARD CAPITAL

Today, St. Petersburg is considered America's shuffleboard capital. Its Mirror Lake Club has more than 100 courts.

Con Artists, Politicians, and a Killer Hurricane

SWAMP SALESMAN

In the 1960s, 1970s, and 1980s, many retirees and other prospective homeowners invested their life savings in lots in what were promoted as pleasant, sun-filled Florida subdivisions, only to arrive and find those lots covered with water, with no prospect of drainage. These people were victims of ruthless, wealthy companies that were eventually convicted of fraud.

However, the practice of selling worthless Florida swampland was nothing new. It dated back more than half a century. The first swamp salesman was a New York con man named Richard Bolles.

Bolles's career as a swindler began shortly after the turn of the 20th century, when he was in his mid-20s. After gaining a seat on the New York Stock Exchange and making a fortune, he moved west, where he made more millions selling ranches in Colorado and Oregon.

Draining the Everglades

At that time the ecological importance of the Everglades was unknown and, as preposterous as it seems today, the state planned to drain what was then thought of as an enormous, worthless swamp. Its rich bottom muck-lands would become some of the best farmland on earth, and its vast acreage would provide land on which to build whole towns and subdivisions. Unfortunately, the plan was successful in the beginning, and much of the Everglades was permanently destroyed.

Governor Napoleon Bonaparte Broward, a strong proponent of drainage, ran into trouble when landowners sued to prevent the levying of a drainage tax. Broward's only recourse was to resort to the sale of public lands. In 1908, Richard Bolles moved to Florida, far away from his disillusioned customers in the West, and bought 500,000 acres of Everglades land for $1 million, with the understanding that half of them would be drained. As he made payments over the next eight years, Bolles would resell these properties as the state drained them. He organized the Florida Fruit Lands Company and planned a massive nationwide promotion to sell the first 180,000 acres as individual lots.

More Hucksters

Bolles's salesmen toured the Midwest, touting the Everglades as a "tropical paradise." They offered inducements such as prizes, lotteries for prime land, and low monthly payments. Bolles proposed a model community, which he called Progresso, in what is Fort Lauderdale today. He touted the area around Lake Okeechobee as a place where families could live in prosperity and comfort by earning a good livelihood from the rich farmland. Prospective buyers flocking in from the North and the Midwest were transported from Fort Myers and Fort Lauderdale aboard Bolles's two steamboats to his hotel at Ritta, where they were given a tour of a carefully laid out model farm. Other companies followed suit, buying and reselling more land. By 1911, at least 50 Chicago real estate companies were selling worthless Florida swampland.

The beginning of the end came on October 15, 1911, when a Washington, D.C., newspaper ran an exposé claiming the entire Everglades drainage program was a sham, designed to deceive gullible out-of-state investors. On investigating further, buyers learned that their lots were still covered with water. Mosquitoes swarmed in the millions, and the marshy land was fit to be inhabited by only insects, snakes, frogs, and scorpions. In Kansas City, a group of buyers brought a civil suit against Bolles to cancel their sales contracts. He was indicted for fraud, but died before he could be brought to trial.

Lawsuits, congressional investigations, and grand-jury indictments temporarily put a stop to the sale of swampland. But the practice reemerged several decades later, on an even grander scale, and resulted in the indictment of such commercial giants as the Gulf American Corporation. In 1970, Robert J. Haiman, managing editor of the *St. Petersburg Times*, wrote: "The sale of Florida swampland to unsuspecting Northerners has long been a national joke. But it's not funny. It's a national scandal."

FEMALE MAYOR

In 1917, before women had the right to vote, and long before it was respectable for a woman to enter politics, the little town of Moore Haven, Florida, had the first lady mayor in the nation.

Marian Horwitz, daughter of a wealthy northern railroad official, was a woman far ahead of her time who was not concerned with what others thought of her. She had come to Florida after the death of her husband, George, to check on some of his land holdings near Lake Okeechobee. A sophisticated world traveler, she was strangely out of place in the small city on the edge of the Everglades. Once there, however, she met and fell in love with John O'Brien, a blustery Irishman who had a way of antagonizing nearly everyone he met. Horwitz decided to stay and make Moore Haven her home. After forming a business partnership with O'Brien, she opened a general store and a bank and served as the head of both. She also became president of her late husband's former company, De Soto Stock Farms.

War Threatens

The imminence of World War I caused a money panic, and a large land company that owned 2 million acres of Everglades land began to sell it in small plots. Farms and small homesteads sprang up around the lake. By August 1917, a half-million additional acres had been drained, leaving rich, black muck that made for excellent farmland. Despite the war, Moore Haven flourished, and was soon incorporated as the first town in the Everglades, with Marian Horwitz serving as mayor. Stores, homes, schools, and churches were built, and the town continued to grow.

Horwitz seemed possessed of boundless energy. It was as if she looked on the development of Moore Haven as a mission. By persuading the Atlantic Coast Line Railroad to come through the town, she made it the center of the huge Lake Okeechobee catfish industry. She worked long hours on her farm, and shipped thousands of bushels of potatoes and other vegetables. Under her leadership, Moore Haven prospered.

Loss of Favor

When Horwitz married John O'Brien during her tenure as mayor, however, she dropped out of favor with the townspeople. The two made a flamboyant pair, and they did not hide the fact that they considered themselves superior to the fishermen, farmers, and other common folk of Moore Haven. Tempers were already inflamed by the bickering of rival land companies, but the O'Briens were the main targets of resentment. Angry townspeople even fired shots at them from behind bushes. When Mayor Marian O'Brien formed a vigilante group to catch the offenders, she became a pariah in the community. She resigned as mayor, and the O'Briens moved 18 miles away to the new settlement of Sand Point, where Marian would build a new town.

Just as she had done in Moore Haven, she built up the town and persuaded the railroad to bring its line to Sand Point. She obtained financial backing from a banker named A. C. Clewis, then hired a Bostonian, John Nolan, to design the new city, which she renamed Clewiston. Today Clewiston is one of the world's largest producers of refined sugar.

USE OF "MIDDLE OF THE ROAD"

The phrase "middle of the road" can be used to describe a politician who avoids extremism and practices fair-mindedness to all, or it can refer to an indecisive fence-sitter. When Albert Gilchrist coined the term in a 1908 bid for governor of Florida, voters must have interpreted it the first way. At

Governor Albert W. Gilchrist led the state from 1909 to 1913. *Courtesy of the Florida State Archives*

any rate, he won the election and served as chief executive of the state from 1909 to 1913.

Gilchrist, the least known of four candidates, emphasized his obscurity to project the image of a candidate who was not beholden to anyone. When accused of fence-straddling, he countered by saying that he wished to be fair and unbiased in all his dealings. His rhetoric included such innocuous phrases as "I will be governor and will surely protect the interests of all classes." He took a firm stand on only one issue, Prohibition, advocating that each county make its own choice, rather than giving the power to the state. Of course, this was also the position of the more populous, "wet" areas of Jacksonville and Tampa.

The Peacemaker

Gilchrist took pains to avoid controversy. When labeled a "little pin-headed governor" for failing to take decisive action against land sharks selling worthless swampland, he countered by saying his critics simply opposed the "progress" of reclaiming the Everglades. He claimed he saw "no undue violence" when an organizing strike by Tampa cigar workers resulted in two lynchings.

In 1916, when the retired governor made his last bid for public office by running for the U.S. Senate, voters decided "the middle of the road" was not the best place to be. Gilchrist was soundly defeated.

THIRD-PARTY CANDIDATE TO BE ELECTED GOVERNOR

When Sidney J. Catts was elected governor of Florida in 1916, he was the state's first third-party candidate ever to hold that office. Catts, a former real estate salesman and a Baptist preacher in Alabama, had few qualifications for high political office, and schooled politicians considered his

Governor Sidney J. Catts rides his Model T in triumph after his election. *Courtesy of the Florida State Archives*

candidacy a joke. While his opponent in the Democratic primary, state treasurer William V. Knotts, campaigned in the cities, Catts chose to use his Model T Ford to take his campaign to the people in Florida's rural areas and small towns. Most of these people had never seen a gubernatorial candidate, but, Catts reasoned, there were a lot more of them, and their votes counted just as much as the city dwellers'. He was the first gubernatorial candidate to use an automobile in his campaign.

Twenty-eight years of preaching had given Catts an eloquent yet simple style that, along with his common touch, appealed to these potential rural voters. Needing a platform on which to base his campaign, he took advantage of growing anti-Catholic sentiment in the state. He equipped his Model T with a loudspeaker and rode from town to town, spreading a message of prejudice and fear, of hatred for Jews and blacks, and especially for Catholics. On dusty dirt roads he crisscrossed the state, going into every rural area and small town he could find. There were few he missed.

A Loud Campaign

As his aide, Jerry Carter, passed out candy and campaign fliers, Catts rode in the back seat with his bullhorn, shouting to mesmerized audiences: "The poor man has only three friends: Jesus Christ, Sears and Roebuck, and Sidney J. Catts." Brandishing the guns he wore on both hips, he loudly proclaimed that the Catholic Church had spent $180,000 to defeat him and had threatened his life. He expounded on the "growing Catholic menace" and promised that as governor he would rid the state of monasteries and nunneries.

On June 6, returns from the first primary were close, with Catts the winner by about 5,000 votes. After his opponent, Knotts, ordered a recount, the Florida Supreme Court declared Knotts the winner by 21 votes. This stirred up a hornet's nest of protest. Many of Catts's former detractors felt he had won fairly and switched their loyalty to him. The Prohibition Party, seeing the rising support for Catts, asked him to be its nominee, and Catts accepted. He declared himself "the people's nominee," while Knotts was "the Court's nominee." Catts continued to campaign with his loudspeaker and Model T, often whipping crowds into a frenzy, convincing them that the court's action was designed to discredit him and withdraw the vote from anti-Catholics. It worked. Catts was elected.

JUST KIDDING

Sidney J. Catts seemed to have no objection to the fact that his secretary in the governor's office was a Catholic, or that one of his sons married one.

Appreciation

When it was time to show appreciation to the voters, Catts again rode from town to town in the back seat of his Model T. This time it was festooned with ribbons and a banner that read "This is the Ford that got me there."

Fortunately, Catts never fulfilled his promise to wipe out Florida's Catholics, and his reign as governor was unspectacular. He was, however, accused of nepotism as he handed out government jobs to friends and family. By the time Catts left office, voters had had enough. He was defeated in a bid for the U.S. Senate in 1920 and in two more tries for the governorship in 1924 and 1928.

CATEGORY 5 HURRICANE TO HIT LAND

When a monster hurricane roared across the Florida Keys on Labor Day 1935, it was the first Category 5 storm ever to hit land in the Western

A restaurant and gas station destroyed by the 1935 hurricane that hit the Florida Keys. *Courtesy of the Florida State Archives*

Hemisphere. How bad is a Category 5 hurricane? This one, unnamed because the practice of naming hurricanes didn't begin until 1952, had tidal waves 18 feet high that swept houses and concrete buildings into the sea. From examining twisted steel rails, huge, uprooted trees, and railroad crossties that had been torn in half, engineers determined that winds had exceeded 250 miles per hour. It was stronger than Hurricane Hugo in 1989, which washed out part of South Carolina. Even the notorious Hurricane Andrew, which caused more than $26 billion worth of damage in 1992 and left thousands homeless, did not equal this storm in intensity or approach it in the number of lives lost. (Hugo and Andrew were Category 4 storms.)

Plans to Evacuate

On Sunday, September 1, 1935, storm warnings were posted for all of southern Florida. From Miami to Key West, people began boarding up their homes and businesses and moving their boats to safety.

On Monday morning, the sky was overcast and the sea was rough. As barometers in the Keys dropped steadily, plans were made to evacuate men who were working on the railroad bridge to Key West in upper and lower Matecumbe Keys. These men were among the 700 World War I veterans who had been dispatched there by President Franklin Roosevelt for a work project. They had been housed in three tent camps, fed three meals a day, and paid $30 a month. Since they had just been paid and now had a three-day weekend because of the Labor Day holiday, about half the workers had left for Miami. They were the fortunate ones.

Before the real danger hit, a train was supposed to leave from Homestead to pick up the men who remained in the Keys. But for some reason still unexplained, no train arrived. A call was made to Miami to send one down. What with delays and red tape, it was 5 P.M., with the storm rapidly intensifying, before the train finally left Homestead and began its journey across a single track through the Everglades and into the Keys.

The train was slowed by high winds. The crew often had to get out and clear trees that had fallen onto the tracks. By 8:30 that night, more than three hours after it had left Homestead, the train reached Islamorada, only 45 miles away. Suddenly, huge, surging winds tossed its 10 cars off the track and onto their sides, ending any chance of rescuing the stranded veterans.

A Night of Horror

What followed was a night of horror. As houses were washed away, people looked in vain for shelter. Many clung to mangrove trees. One man tied his wife and five children together with rope to form a human chain. Miraculously, they survived.

The next day, the devastation was everywhere. Several families living in the Keys had been swept away, and their bodies were never recovered. Others lost their homes and all their possessions. One family found its house a mile away, where it had been washed onto the beach of another island. Whole islands disappeared.

The search for the dead began in earnest. Some were found in mangrove swamps; others floated in Florida Bay, or washed up on the islands. Because the islands were small and the surrounding seas so vast, most victims were never found. Many of the corpses were mangled

---

RECORDS

The hurricane of 1935 set two records. One was for winds of over 250 miles per hour. The other was for the lowest barometer reading ever recorded on land anywhere in the world. At several weather stations in the Keys, barometers dropped to 26.35 inches.

beyond recognition. Rescue workers could not identify bodies fast enough in the scorching heat, so authorities, fearing a health crisis, ordered them piled up and cremated. The death toll, officially listed as 408, was undoubtedly much higher.

LATTER-DAY HURRICANES

In 1999, Hurricane Floyd, a Category 5 storm, threatened to strike Florida's east coast in its full fury. In one of the largest migrations in history, thousands evacuated their homes. But the monstrous storm unexpectedly veered north. When Floyd hit North Carolina the next day, it had diminished to a Category 4 hurricane. Only one other Category 5 storm, Hurricane Camille, which destroyed parts of Mississippi and Louisiana in 1969, has ever struck the United States.

SAFE FROM SHARKS

The world's first effective shark repellent was developed in Florida during World War II. Marine Studios, working with the U.S. government, found a way to protect servicemen who became stranded in the water after their ships were sunk. Poured in the water, the repellent would keep sharks at bay for up to six hours.

Leisure and Lifestyle

SPORT SHIRT

Addison Mizner, the renowned but eccentric architect, is well known for the role he played in the development of southern Florida. Few know, however, that he also wore America's first sport shirt.

In the 1920s, Mizner was in demand by wealthy residents of Palm Beach as the designer of many of its stunning, Mediterranean-style public buildings and luxurious private homes. Later he built the Boca Raton Hotel and Club in a town that he expected to rival Palm Beach for elegance.

A Mizner mansion was the ultimate status symbol. So unique was his work that even mistakes were hailed as innovations. He once built a house, only to discover that he had left out the staircase because he failed to include it in the floor plans. He hurriedly added an outdoor, spiral stairway to the finished house, designing it to be a thing of beauty. Other clients demanded that their homes also be built with the stairs outside.

A Fashion Trendsetter

Because he weighed nearly 300 pounds, Mizner found the high-buttoned collars worn in public by gentlemen of the day to be extremely confining. He took to strolling tony Worth Avenue with his shirt collar open and his shirttail outside his trousers. In fashion-conscious Palm Beach, a man of lesser stature would have been ostracized for his sloppiness. But just as he had done in the buildings he designed, Mizner made his own rules about his personal life. Undoubtedly he only wanted to be comfortable and had no interest in setting a trend, but that is exactly what he did.

Other men decided they, too, had a right to be comfortable and imitated Mizner's "style." As demand grew for less-formal clothing, Palm Beach designers created short-sleeved, open-collared shirts that could be worn tucked in or untucked, and the sport shirt was born.

BRIDGE PHONE TO REDUCE SUICIDES

A young man, distraught over his failing marriage, parked his pickup truck at the crest of the Sunshine Skyway Bridge, walked to the railing, put one leg over it, then paused to reconsider. He picked up a red, solar-powered telephone and called for help. A specially trained counselor from the Crisis Center of Hillsborough County answered the call, and another counselor notified the Florida Highway Patrol.

The phone was one of six installed on the bridge in 1999. While phones had already been installed on the Golden Gate Bridge in San Francisco, they rang only to the bridge authority. The Sunshine Skyway phones are the first to ring directly to a crisis center.

Beautiful but Deadly

While the bridge is one of the most beautiful in the nation, it is also among the most deadly, with the third-highest suicide rate. Only the Golden Gate and San Diego's Coronado Bridge rank higher. Since 1996, 26 people have died jumping from the Sunshine Skyway Bridge, most from its crest, 197 feet above Tampa Bay, where two phones were installed. The other four were placed on the concrete supports that hold up the cables before and after the crest, as some people had jumped from there.

While the phones won't stop all would-be suicides, they are expected to deter those who have second thoughts. "The purpose of the phones is for the crisis center to convince [people] there is another way out," said Sergeant Harold Winsett, head of the crisis negotiating team of the Hillsborough County Sheriff's Office. "This gives them another option."

ELVIS PRESLEY RIOT

The frenzy was building. Teenaged girl fans in Daytona and Orlando had squealed and screamed over the newest 20-year-old singing, guitar-playing, hip-swinging sensation. But when Elvis Presley wound up his 1955 Florida tour at Jacksonville's Gator Bowl, the unassuming former truck driver nearly had to fight to stay alive. It was the first of many riots after a Presley concert.

At the end of his act, before an audience of 14,000 fans shouting unsubtle come-ons, Presley rolled his eyes and dropped what he thought was a harmless, playful remark. "Girls," he said, "I'll see ya'll backstage."

They Took Him Literally

It took a police escort to get Presley to the locker room. He soon found himself in the midst of screaming girls, who had found their way in through an unlocked window. They began grabbing at Elvis and tearing his clothes off, shredding his shirt and ripping his coat to pieces. With nothing but his pants on, he managed to make his way to the top of a shower stall, where he crouched, bewildered, as the girls attempted to grab his only remaining article of clothing.

When the tour left Florida and continued on to other cities, Presley was careful not to make statements his fans might take as an invitation. To discourage riots, an announcer came onstage after each concert to say, "Elvis has left the building." But it was too late. The wild frenzy of that night in Jacksonville marked Elvis concerts from that time on.

AMERICAN PRINCESS

In America, where many a small girl has dreamed of someday becoming the bride of a prince, more than a few have actually done it. The first American girl to become a bona fide princess was a beautiful, young Tallahassee widow named Catherine Willis Gray. On July 30, 1826, Gray was joined in marriage to Prince Charles Louis Napoleon Achille Murat of France.

Murat was a nephew of Napoleon Bonaparte and the son of Joachim, king of Naples from 1808 to 1815. After his father was killed by his once-devoted subjects, Murat came to America. He traveled the new country extensively, then settled in the little village of Tallahassee and rented a small log cabin, which soon became a center for social activities in Florida's new capital. It was here that the titled Frenchman, then 26 years old, met and instantly fell in love with 23-year-old Catherine Gray.

At first, Catherine was not impressed with Murat. Despite his royal title, for which he cared little, Murat dressed in the homespun manner of the backwoods cowboys, chewed tobacco, and bathed infrequently. The fastidious Catherine, accustomed to gentlemen with impeccable backgrounds and bearing, considered him beneath her station. She was the daughter of George Washington's niece, and her family had been Virginia aristocrats. Murat, on the other hand, was the grandson of an obscure French innkeeper; it was only recently that his family had become royalty.

But Murat was persistent, and gradually Catherine began to notice other qualities beneath the rough exterior. Murat had a brilliant mind and a rare stability. He was truly devoted to her, and she had a strong sense that he always would be. She began to feel the same devotion for him, and over time the feeling grew stronger. She married for love and never regretted her decision.

Before the marriage, Murat had bought Lipona, a plantation 20 miles from Tallahassee. Here the couple lived a simple but happy life until Murat, still a Frenchman at heart, heard of trouble in France, with the threat of the dissolution of the monarchy.

Concerned that such an action would void his claim to a fortune of several million francs, he pawned the plantation and left with Catherine for his native country. After three years of futile efforts to claim the money, the couple returned to find the plantation in a terrible state of disrepair.

After losing money on speculative business deals, then being completely wiped out by the Panic of 1837, which destroyed banks and businesses in the United States, Murat went back to Europe to attempt to claim his fortune. Once again he failed, and returned to Tallahassee. He and Catherine lived in near-poverty until he fell ill and died in 1847, at the age of 46. Catherine moved to a small house in town, where she lived until her death 20 years later.

CHILD TO DIVORCE PARENT

When a judge in a courtroom in central Florida granted Gregory Kingsley a divorce from Rachel Kingsley in 1992, it was a landmark decision. Gregory was 12 years old, and Rachel was his mother.

It wasn't the first time a child had legally severed ties with a parent, but in previous cases it had been an adult, usually a foster parent or an official of the state, who hired the attorney and pursued the lawsuit. This time, Gregory had engaged his own lawyer and initiated the suit himself. It was the first time in the United States that a minor had been granted independent legal status to sue his parents.

Gregory testified in court that years would go by without his hearing from his mother, that she never remembered Christmas or birthdays, and that he had lived with her only seven months in the last eight years. "I just thought she forgot about me," he said. His parents were separated, and for brief periods during those years he had lived with his natural father. The rest of the time, he had lived in foster homes.

A New Life

Gregory was living in a state-run home for boys in Lake County when he was spotted by George Russ, a local attorney visiting on a routine inspection. Something about the boy struck a responsive chord in Russ, a father of eight. A few weeks later he brought his wife, Lizabeth, to meet Gregory, and the two of them decided to ask if they could bring him home as a foster child. In October 1991, after foster-parent training and several weekend visits, the Russes became Gregory's official foster parents.

After living with the Russes for a year, Gregory began to ask questions about adoption by George and Lizabeth Russ. Because Gregory had not heard from Rachel at all since he had begun living with them, the Russes assumed they would have no trouble adopting him. They were shocked to learn that neither of Gregory's natural parents would agree to relinquish custody.

A few months later, Gregory's natural father changed his mind and agreed to surrender his parental rights. But Rachel Kingsley hired a lawyer and fought the charges that she was an unfit mother. She claimed she loved her child, that poverty and other unfortunate circumstances had prevented her from giving him the care and attention he needed. She was, she said, now able to care for her son, and she wanted him back. She charged that the Russes had overstepped their bounds as foster parents.

Gregory clearly did not want to go back to his mother and asked Russ if there was something he could do to prevent it. Russ gave Gregory the name of another attorney, Jerri Blair, but insisted that Gregory be the one to call and instigate the lawsuit. Blair agreed to represent her young client without payment.

Victory

When Judge Thomas Kirk made his ruling in the case, he declared: "Gregory, you are the son of Mr. and Mrs. Russ at this moment." Tears and

ANOTHER CASE

George Russ again made headlines in 1993, when he agreed to represent Kimberly Mays, a 14-year-old girl who had been switched at birth with the sickly child of another family, Ernest and Regina Twigg. The Twiggs lost their parental rights to Kimberly, who shortly after the ruling decided to move in with them anyway.

hugs greeted the verdict as Gregory—or Shawn Russ, as he now preferred to be called—embraced his new family.

Fears that the ruling might bring on a spate of frivolous lawsuits by disgruntled kids who were forced to clean their rooms or forgo Nintendo games were unfounded. Instead, the ruling made a positive statement that children are not second-class citizens, nor are they the chattel of their parents. Children, like everyone else, have rights and must be allowed to pursue them.

WILD-ANIMAL ATTRACTION

When the Clyde Beatty Jungle Zoo opened in 1939, it was Fort Lauderdale's first major tourist attraction and the first such attraction in the United States to present acts featuring large wild animals.

Clyde Beatty, a well-known animal trainer, had been touring with the Cole Brothers–Clyde Beatty circus in 1938 when a disastrous season forced it into bankruptcy. When an investment company foreclosed a mortgage on the circus property and took possession of the animals, Beatty bought all the lions and tigers and three elephants from the company.

Profitable Vacation

That winter, while on a vacation in Florida, Beatty spotted an unusual sight as he drove along U.S. Route 1 just north of Fort Lauderdale: the McKillop-Hutton Lion Farm, which had been established in 1935 on the site of an abandoned rock pit and specialized in breeding and training lions for circuses and zoos. When Beatty got out to look around, he found an employee working with five lions in flimsy cages made of chicken wire.

Beatty returned the following spring and bought out the farm, as well as some of the surrounding land. He spent about $85,000 constructing a site to resemble an African veld, complete with grottoes, a waterfall, and false mountains. When it was finished, the Clyde Beatty Jungle Zoo was a sight to behold, with beautiful landscaping, two tree-shaded lagoons, and graceful flamingos, pheasants, peacocks, and cranes wandering along garden paths. And animals—monkeys, lions, tigers, elephants, alligators, and black bears—were everywhere. During the 1939 Christmas season, when Santa Claus arrived in Fort Lauderdale on a Florida East Coast train, he was greeted at the station by three Clyde Beatty elephants. Santa then delighted the children of the city by riding an elephant through the business district.

Rise and Fall

The zoo was an immediate success and attracted thousands of visitors to southern Florida, bringing nationwide publicity to Fort Lauderdale. The circus consisted of 10 acts that were presented two, sometimes three, times daily. It had clowns, aerialists, and performing chimpanzees. Beatty's wife, Harriet, presented a lion-and-tiger team riding the elephant Annie Mae. The highlight of the show was Clyde presenting his big mixed-cat act.

Clyde and Harriet Beatty, who were in their 30s when they moved to Fort Lauderdale, loved the city and built a house there, planning to stay for the rest of their lives. Unfortunately, that was not to be.

While the zoo had been two miles outside town when it opened, it was now surrounded by business and residential development. Nearby residents complained of blaring loudspeakers, screeching monkeys, and crying peacocks. They also claimed that some monkeys had escaped and terrified the residents. And the lions, they said, disturbed their peace by roaring at night.

Beatty tried to appease them. He sold his peacocks at a loss and toned down the loudspeaker so it could be heard only on the grounds. Unfortunately, he couldn't do anything about the lions.

The neighbors' complaints grew into threats of lawsuits. City officials argued that the zoo had been there first and residents knew about it when they bought their properties. Also, the zoo and the Beatty name had brought much valuable publicity to the city. Beatty said he had invested $125,000 in the property and couldn't afford to move.

But the outspoken minority finally got its way. Reluctantly, the city commission gave in and passed a law prohibiting the keeping of wild animals within the city limits. The Beattys were forced to sell their house, take their animals, and leave.

Harriet Beatty died of a heart ailment in 1950 and was buried in Fort Lauderdale, as per her wishes. Clyde Beatty brought his circus back to the city for one-day stands almost every year. In 1960, he opened Clyde Beatty's Jungleland near Hollywood, Florida, but it lasted for only one season. "It's my firm belief," Beatty predicted, "that I'll continue working in the arena as long as I can get around." The prediction held true until Beatty died of cancer in 1965. He was 62 years old.

ADVENTURE NOVEL

America's first adventure novel was a true narrative by Jonathan Dickinson, who, along with his family and several companions, was shipwrecked off the Florida coast in 1696 near what is now Hobe Sound. It was first published in 1699 and given the title *God's Protecting Providence, Man's*

Surest Help and Defence in Times of Greatest Difficulty, Evidenced in the Remarkable Deliverance of Robert Barrow from the Cruel Devouring Jaws of the Inhuman Cannibals of Florida.

Dickinson's voyage started on August 23, 1696, when he left Jamaica with his wife, Mary, and their six-month-old baby boy in their small barkentine, the *Reformation*. Along with two other white passengers, 10 slaves, an Indian girl, and a crew of nine, the family headed for Philadelphia.

Shipwreck

As they sailed by the Florida coast, a storm struck and wrecked their ship, washing it ashore on Jupiter Island. Hostile Indians took the party captive, but later released them.

The Dickinson party then set out on foot for Charleston, South Carolina, 600 miles away. Dickinson kept a journal throughout the four-month trip, during which the travelers were again captured by Indians and often went days without food. Five members of the party died, but the Dickinsons and their son survived. *God's Protecting Providence* records the story of their capture and gives an account of the everyday lives of their captors. It tells of the hardships they faced on their journey and of how they were ultimately released at St. Augustine.

Dickinson and his family moved on to Philadelphia, where he published the journal. It instantly became a bestseller in both America and England. After becoming a successful merchant in Philadelphia, the reluctant adventurer was elected mayor of the city.

Jonathan Dickinson State Park, near Hobe Sound, has preserved the land as it was in the days of the famous shipwreck. Wildlife and bird watchers can see dozens of species of animals and birds in the 11,300-acre park. Visitors can rent a canoe or take a guided tour on an excursion boat $4^1/_2$ miles up the Loxahatchee River, the only National Wild and Scenic River in Florida.

☼ *To Visit: Jonathan Dickinson State Park*

Jonathan Dickinson State Park
16450 Southeast Federal Highway (U.S. Route 1)
Hobe Sound, FL 33455
561-546-2771
Hours: Daily, 8 A.M.-sundown
Admission charged.

BERTRAM 31 POWERBOAT

The now legendary Bertram 31 powerboat was first produced in a rented Hialeah warehouse in 1960. When it was introduced at the New York National Boat Show in 1961, it launched the Bertram Yacht company and the advent of the modern powerboat with its fiberglass construction, deep V design, stern drives, and larger engines.

Miami yacht broker Richard Bertram was competing in the 1958 America's Cup trials in Rhode Island when he noticed a small boat slicing through the rough waters, aided by an unusual V-shaped bottom. When Bertram learned the designer was C. Raymond Hunt, he tracked Hunt down and commissioned him to build a larger version so Bertram could commute from his waterfront home to his downtown office. He named the 30-foot boat *Moppie*, after his wife, and entered it in the 1960 Miami–Nassau powerboat race.

A Winner

The boat won the race, breaking the course record. Its nearest competitor, which came in two hours later, was also a boat with a deep V hull, the only other one in the race. Because of rough weather and choppy seas, the other boats were forced to return to port or come back the next day to finish. "It changed the face of yachting forever," said Jim Martenhoff, an ocean racer and former boating editor for the *Miami Herald.* "No other event has had as great an impact on powerboating as the 1960 Miami–Nassau race."

Bertram had a mold cast from *Moppie* and created the first fiberglass Bertram 31. In 1961, he again won the Miami–Nassau race, this time in *Glass Moppie*, the fiberglass version of the original.

The Bertram 31 was bought by lovers of the sea all over the world, and many are still operating. Before 1977, when the molds were retired, 1,860 Bertram 31s had been sold. Today the boat is a collectible classic.

SUGGESTED READINGS

Blashfield, Jean F., and Cima Star. *Awesome Almanac: Florida*. Walworth, Wis.: B&B Publishing, 1994.

Brotemarkle, Benjamin. *Beyond the Theme Parks: Exploring Central Florida*. Gainesville: University Press of Florida, 1999.

Brown, Warren J. *Florida's Aviation History: The First 100 Years*. Largo, Fla.: Aero-Medical Consultants, 1994.

Burnett, Gene M. *Florida's Past: People and Events That Shaped the State*. 3 vols. Sarasota: Pineapple Press, 1991.

Burt, Al. *Al Burt's Florida: Snowbirds, Sand Castles, and Self-Rising Crackers*. Gainesville: University Press of Florida, 1998.

Derr, Mark. *Some Kind of Paradise: A Chronicle of Man and the Land in Florida*. Gainesville: University Press of Florida, 1998.

Douglas, Marjory Stoneman. *The Everglades: River of Grass*. Anniversary ed. Sarasota: Pineapple Press, 1997.

———. *Florida: The Long Frontier*. New York: Harper & Row, 1967.

Gannon, Michael. *Florida: A Short History*. Gainesville: University Press of Florida, 1993.

———. *The New History of Florida*. Gainesville: University Press of Florida, 1996.

Jahoda, Gloria. *Florida—A History*. New York: W.W. Norton, 1976.

———. *The Other Florida*. New York: Charles Scribner's Sons, 1967.

Shofner, Jerrell. *Florida Portrait: A Pictorial History of Florida*. Sarasota: Pineapple Press, 1990.

Tebeau, Charlton W. *A History of Florida*. Coral Gables: University of Miami Press, 1971.